KATHARINE HILL

IF YOU **FORGET** EVERYTHING ELSE **REMEMBER** THIS

PARENTING IN THE PRIMARY YEARS

Muddy
Pearl

First published in 2015 by
Muddy Pearl, Edinburgh, Scotland.
www.muddypearl.com
books@muddypearl.com

Third printing 2016

British Library Cataloguing in Publication Data
A catalogue record for this book is available from the British Library
ISBN 978-1-910012-25-3

Typeset in Minion by Revo Creative Ltd, Carlisle, Cumbria
Printed in Great Britain by Bell & Bain Ltd, Glasgow

To Jo, Jane and Ginny – fourteen children between us – thanks for your friendship and support during the ups and downs of the primary years!

ACKNOWLEDGEMENTS

This book has been a lot of fun to write – a heartfelt thank you to all those who have helped make it possible. Huge thanks to Rob Parsons for his wisdom, help and encouragement, and for writing the Foreword.

Thank you to the amazing team at Care for the Family – especially to Paula Pridham and Sheron Rice for their comments on the manuscript and also to Samantha Callan.

Thank you to Stephanie and Richard Heald at Muddy Pearl – for your care, creativity and attention to detail – it has been great working with you. And to David McNeill for the wonderful cartoons that make me laugh out loud.

And the biggest thank you to Richard and to our four children: George, Charlotte, Ed and Henry – without whom the book couldn't possibly have been written!

CONTENTS

FOREWORD

Last month our washing machine stopped working. That little event sent me trawling through the kitchen drawers looking for the instruction manual that I was sure that I had put 'somewhere safe.' When I eventually found it I discovered that somebody had torn off the pages that were in English and left me with a choice of Spanish or Mandarin.

It was frustrating, but I can tell you that there were times in our parenting that I'd have settled for an instruction manual in any language. In fact I wish that my wife, Dianne, and I had owned a copy of *Remember This* when our kids were small. In this wonderful book Katharine tackles the big issues that affect every parent of primary age children. But this is not just another parenting book – *Remember This* oozes wisdom, practical help and above all – understanding. There are times in all our parenting when we wish that either we could have another go at it – or at least that there was somewhere we could go to discover help with the everyday challenges – and blessings of being a mum or a dad. How can we give our children strong roots that will help them face the storms of life – not to mention the trauma of the teenage years? How should we deal with the testing toddler who tries us daily? What is the best way to set (and enforce!) boundaries? How can we get our children ready for the world out there – so they can stand on their own two feet? How do our children come to believe that they are loved? Katharine tackles these issues – and a dozen more.

This book made me laugh (the cartoons are brilliant!), and at times it moved me greatly, but I think what I love most about it is that it's so very down to earth. We need answers to some of the dilemmas we face as parents – and *Remember This* gives us those, but even more important is the life-changing, liberating news that we are not alone: even if we are struggling a bit at this stage of our parenting – others have worn that tee-shirt and come through it. And Katharine has worn the tee-shirt – but not just as a mum of four but somebody who has spoken to – and perhaps even more importantly – listened to – thousands of parents.

Enjoy it.

Rob Parsons
February 2015

INTRODUCTION

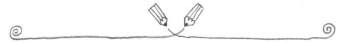

Twenty-six years ago today was the day that changed everything. I became a parent. After the elation of seeing the pregnancy test turn blue, followed by months of enduring what is commonly known as 'morning' sickness (a misnomer if ever there was one), I was looking forward with excitement to my first child's arrival. Nothing, however, prepared me for what was to follow.

The week before, I'd had a busy full-time job and (with the exception of the morning sickness) felt fully in control of my world. But at thirty-seven weeks pregnant, rock and rolling with my husband, Richard, at a friend's wedding seemed to be all that was needed to kick-start the onset of labour, and eight hours later I found myself gazing at the little red and wrinkled bundle that was our son.

What I didn't know was the extent to which life was about to change ... forever. This baby had taken longer to conceive than I had imagined, and the monthly roller coaster of hope and anticipation followed by crashing disappointment had become an unwelcome but familiar routine. I naïvely assumed that the struggle to conceive, eight-and-a-half months of nausea followed by a night of hard labour meant that the difficult bit was over, and looked forward to life as a mummy with a mixture of excitement and anticipation. I had had antenatal advice by the bucketload on the practical challenges of the first few weeks – feeding, bathing, changing – all mastered whilst enduring acute sleep deprivation which seemed to put Special Forces training in the shade.

Useful as that was, my focus on the few weeks following the birth meant that I had somehow overlooked the fact that this was just the beginning. The journey of parenthood had really only just begun. If I thought that babies and toddlers were challenging, that was only because I hadn't yet tried to get a four-year-old unstuck from a lamp-post and into his first day at school, stayed up till the small hours trying to make my son a Bart Simpson mask for the school play 'like Jonny's mummy can make', or realised that my ten-year-old was serious when he told me that his classmate, Charlie 'knew where he could get weed' – and he wasn't referring to the classroom allotment.

In the whirlwind of life as a parent, for not one or two but eventually for four primary age children (*what* were we thinking?), amidst the chaos of finding swimming goggles, making packed lunches, cleaning out the rabbit, refereeing sibling squabbles, de-lousing hair and mending broken laces, what I have longed for (other than a good night's sleep and a some adult conversation) was a book that I could pick up quickly and easily to find some wisdom to help me navigate this wonderful but challenging season of life. In the same way that the ancient book of Proverbs gives bite-sized principles for living, I needed something that would give me principles for parenting and family life.

I wanted a book of short and to-the-point sayings that I could read in a few minutes while waiting for the kettle to boil – sayings that I could commit to memory and draw upon at a second's notice. This is that book: a series of short chapters offering memorable sayings that will bring direction and clarity to us in our important role as parents and carers. I have tried to make each chapter heading a catchphrase that can be easily recalled in an instant amidst the busyness, tiredness and chaos that go with the territory of parenting in the primary years.

So fill the kettle, make a cup of tea, turn the page, and if you forget everything else as a parent, remember *this* …

FASTEN YOUR SEAT BELTS

Fasten your seatbelts

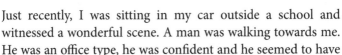

Just recently, I was sitting in my car outside a school and witnessed a wonderful scene. A man was walking towards me. He was an office type, he was confident and he seemed to have it all together. Yet it wasn't a briefcase he was holding, but the hand of a little girl, who looked about four years old.

I watched them as they left the pavement and made their way down the little path towards the school door. They walked a few paces, then he bent and whispered into her ear, and then they walked on a little further. And suddenly it dawned on me: it was her first day at school. As they reached the entrance, I don't know which of them was the most reluctant to let go of the other, but finally she skipped into school with a wave, and a teacher took her hand and led her into her new life. The man waved too and blew a kiss at the closed door. And then he went to a nearby window and I saw him waving again and smiling. I could almost see his chest swell with joy and pride as he watched her in her first classroom. And so all was well – a milestone reached and another child launched successfully into a new season. He turned and began walking back towards me.

And that's when I saw him brush away a tear.

I sat in the car for a moment and thought about the little scene that had just been enacted before my eyes. Of course, in many ways it wasn't special at all – it was being repeated at a thousand school gates all across the country. And yet I knew I had witnessed something profound. The smile, the wave and the tear sums up the incredible task of parenting – fun times, sad times, and, every step of the way, getting ready for the day when we have to let them go.

My mind went back to my son's first day at school and another thought occurred to me. This was just the start. If that father was thinking that moment marked the end of the baby years, and this was the last time he would feel such a swing of emotion, then he was wrong. The weeks, months, and years ahead would be full of waves, smiles and tears, but so much more: times of unimaginable pleasure, fulfilment, laughter and deep joy, closely followed by periods of exhaustion, frustration, guilt and despair … and back again. It goes with the territory of parenthood, even for the most serious and unemotional of grown adults. You will have your heart filled with joy and then broken, and then put back together, again and again. Elizabeth Stone put it well: 'Making the decision to have a child – it is momentous. It is to decide forever to have your heart go walking around outside your body.'

Motherhood and fatherhood is an emotional roller coaster, with ups and downs, joys and challenges, laughter and pain.

Parenting is also a long haul business. Sometimes at Care for the Family events, we ask parents of pre-schoolers to raise their hands. Then we ask them if they are looking forward (just a bit!) to the time when the children are grown and standing on their own two feet. Weary mums and dads raise their hands – and sometimes I can see just the hint of a hope of a day when they won't have to worry about these little ones. When their hands are lowered we ask if there are any parents in the audience with children in their thirties or even forties. There are always some grandparents present who will obligingly raise their hands. Then we ask them, 'Do you still worry about your children?' In the twenty-five years we have been doing this, we have never been disappointed with the answer: 'More than ever!' We then turn to the newer parents and say, 'And that's why you must pace yourself – it really is a long haul business!'

"have a safe trip and enjoy your new life with the little one"

Life as a parent is like a roller coaster – a long haul roller coaster – full of moments of incredible joy, fun and laughter and times of tears, worry and pain. Tantrums, whining and sibling rivalry one minute; an angelic role in the nativity play the next; frantic trips to A&E and anxious minutes in the hospital waiting room; delight at exam success and disappointment at failure, good news and bad news; reassurance at milestones met and gut-wrenching worry at milestones missed; fulfilling friendships, fallings out and school bullies; first loves and broken hearts; financial pressure; flooded campsites and holidays in the sun. And it's something most parents are totally unprepared for, at each new stage! There's nothing else like it – it's the ride of a lifetime – but once you've climbed on board, expect there to be a few ups and downs on the way.

So hold on tight and fasten your seatbelts!

REMEMBER
WHO
YOU
ARE

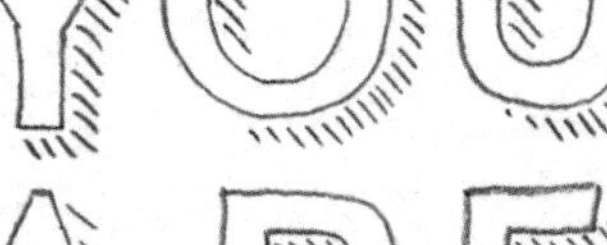

Remember who you are

Donna was a teenage single-parent mum who came to a recent Care for the Family parenting event. She was at least ten years younger than the rest of the women there, and, I confess, I wondered just how helpful the event would be for her. At the end of the evening she came to find me, got out her phone and proudly showed me a picture of her little boy. He was sitting in the bath, covered with bath foam and grinning from ear to ear. What she said next surprised me. She commented that the most helpful bit of the evening was when we spoke about loss of confidence and identity. She had been a student when she had her baby, and she had been catapulted, almost overnight, from her coursework on fashion and design, to the responsibility of parenthood. She said, 'I realised that I was so overwhelmed with being a mum that somewhere along the way I had lost myself. It was such a relief to hear that that was normal and to be encouraged to stop and remember who I am.' This loss of confidence is not simply the preserve of young mums like Donna but seems to engulf mothers everywhere. Mothers, regardless of age, background or life experience find themselves asking the same question: 'Who am I?'

Becoming a parent brings different challenges for both men and women. Many women in particular find that when they become a mum for the first time, their confidence and self-esteem is dealt a surprising blow. We wonder if our bodies will ever return to their pre-baby shape (answer: probably not), and our ability to think clearly or engage in any rational conversation may seem to have deserted us. It can take time for our confidence to return.

The process of regaining confidence after having children can never be a quick fix, but there are practical things we can do that can help us rebuild our confidence and rediscover our identity. Looking back, finding 'child free' moments certainly helped me in the quest. As much as I wholeheartedly embraced this stage of life, and loved being a mum, those moments were a welcome reminder that there was life beyond children. A weekly Mums' Group with a crèche gave an oasis in the week, with an opportunity to make new friends and to engage in adult conversation. A regular arrangement with a friend also paid dividends. I would look after her children one Wednesday

afternoon and she had mine the next. Full blown chaos in the house one week was rewarded on the alternate week with some time to ourselves when we could shop, bath, read, write, tidy the house, watch TV, drink coffee, or sleep, uninterrupted and unencumbered. Bliss! In my experience, this loss of identity[1] is usually the preserve of mums, but some dads also can find the adjustment to the responsibility of parenthood, the change in family priorities (and in their partner!) a challenge. Dads: if you are parenting together, you can help mums in this area by taking the initiative in nurturing your relationship in small ways – a compliment, a small gift or gesture – reaffirming her identity as the woman you love.

There is no shortage of advice as to how to regain this loss of identity and it often involves keeping your hand in at your previous job or career or reminding yourself how successful you once were. One friend suggested that I keep a copy of my professional qualification certificate framed in the loo and look at it daily to remind myself of what I once achieved. Another friend suggested dressing up once a month and meeting old work colleagues to catch up on the latest 'news'. But frankly, these suggestions fail because they fall into the trap of assuming that my identity was based on my previous job and life. But it's not. I am a woman with gifts, hopes and aspirations, whether or not I choose to work mainly inside or outside of the home. My identity isn't in my paid job, as much as I enjoy it, and – much

1 Redrick, Mia. (2012). Huffington Post: *How Women Lose Themselves in Motherhood*. http://www.huffington-post.com/mia-redrick/motherhood_b_1558981.html

to the chagrin of some other parents I meet – it is not in my children either. And, if it was in either of those things, then the day I lost that job or my kids left home I would lose … *me*. No, I decided to put a different poster on the loo wall: 'Katharine, God made you and loved you before your job, before your kids – there is nothing to prove.' (Ok, I didn't *actually* hang it up – but there were times I wish I had!)

Over the years I have been at home as a full-time mum, and I have worked outside the home, both part and full time, I have volunteered, and I have been self-employed and employed. When the children were small and I was at home full time, my husband and I were invited to a smart executive dinner. In my life BC (before children) I would have looked forward to the evening – a chance to dress up, make up and to engage with interesting people, and I would have accepted the invitation immediately. However now things had changed, and I approached the evening with some trepidation. The prospect of arranging a babysitter who could put four children to bed, then squeezing my body into my BC dress were the first two hurdles to overcome. These, however, paled into insignificance in comparison with my anxiety about whether I would be able to engage in interesting conversation, or even have the ability to string a coherent sentence together about anything other than the escaped hamster, the new recipe for Play-Doh or my daughter's new reading book. My fears were not unfounded. Once pre-dinner drinks were successfully negotiated, we were shown to our places. Seated to my right was a BBC producer and to my left a business consultant. As we sat down the consultant turned to me and asked me the question I had been dreading:

'Do you work?'

I mumbled something about being at home with the children, he gave me a kind smile and turned his attention to the lady on his left, with whom I imagine he had a much more interesting conversation. Years later I came across a brilliant answer given by another mum when asked the same question. If only I'd had it then – I'd have given him something to consult about!

Yes – actually – I do work. I'm in a programme of social development. At the moment I'm working with three age groups: firstly with babies and toddlers – which involves a basic grasp of medicine and child psychology, next – teenagers – I confess the programme is not going so well in that area. And finally, in evenings and during weekends, I work with a man aged thirty-nine who is exhibiting all the classic symptoms of mid-life crisis – that's mainly psychiatric work. The whole job involves planning, a 'make-it-happen' attitude and the ability to crisis-manage. I used to be an international fashion model – but I got bored.

There is a wonderful scene in the Disney film *The Lion King*. Simba's wicked uncle, Scar, has tricked the young lion into thinking he is responsible for killing his father, Mufasa, the king. Grief-stricken, Simba flees into exile and leaves behind his identity as the Lion King. Rafiki, the mandrill, befriends him, and, seeking to restore him to the throne, takes him to meet with the spirit of his father. In a reflection from a pool, Mufasa's voice booms from the deep as he speaks to his son, Simba, 'Remember who you are.'

As parents, mums or dads, we would do well to do the same. We have an identity not defined by our roles in the workplace or even by our role as partners or parents, important as those are. We are unique individuals with different gifts and needs, each of whom has been placed on Planet Earth for a purpose. In the turmoil and busyness of family life, particularly in the early days, it's well worth taking just a few moments to … remember who you are.

THERE'S NO POINT TRYING TO BE SUPERMUM (OR SUPERDAD)

I put the finishing touches to the birthday cake and glanced at the kitchen clock. It was 35 minutes past midnight. I stood back to admire my handiwork and had to admit that it was a masterpiece. Rows of miniature coloured icing carrots, radishes, French beans and lettuces were planted in the chocolate icing vegetable patch. A wheelbarrow and garden fork stood nearby, alongside the scarecrow wearing Peter Rabbit's blue jacket and shoes hung there by Mr McGregor. Beatrix Potter herself would have been proud. Everything would be perfect for Charlotte's birthday party.

Years later my friends still laugh about 'The Peter Rabbit cake'. It has gone down in the annals of our friendship, but not for the reasons I would have hoped. The cake incident might possibly have been overlooked if my efforts to emulate Jane Asher had stopped there. But they didn't. I am embarrassed to admit that I recently discovered a photograph album of Hill family themed birthday cakes – Thunderbirds, princesses, castles, forts, dinosaurs, a Mad Hatter's top hat (the *piece de resistance* for an *Alice in Wonderland* themed party complete with fancy dress), boats, cars, pirate chests and many more works of art besides. Apparently in my efforts (born of basement-level self-esteem) I had inadvertently raised the bar and condemned my friends to attempt to do likewise – including creations of Mickey Mouse, the Star Ship Enterprise and more Ninja Turtles than any of them were inclined to remember.

What was I thinking? We laugh about it now, but looking back, I can see that this cake (and others like it!) represented my attempt to be Supermum. I needed to face the uncomfortable truth and ask myself what I was trying to prove, who I was trying to impress, and who the Peter Rabbit cake, the Mad Hatter Cake, and others like it were really for. It certainly wasn't for the four-year-olds at the party, who would have been just as happy with a caterpillar cake from Tesco.

It seems that I am not alone. A recent poll[2] showed that, in their attempts to be Supermum (or Superdad), most parents cannot help but brag about their children's achievements. Facebook news feeds are clogged with status updates about Emily's brilliant starring role as a raindrop in the nativity play or the outstanding goal that Simon nearly scored in the hockey match. Two-thirds of parents say they use Facebook to post status updates about their offspring, and parents polled admitted they were most likely to post statuses boasting about their child's achievements.

Although possibly more an issue for mums, dads can also succumb to the pressure of needing to wear their underpants

2 Female First, *Proud Parents on Facebook* (2014). http://www.femalefirst.co.uk/parenting/proud-parents-on-facebook-400567.html.,The poll was carried out by VoucherCodesPro.co.uk.
A total of 2,204 parents from the UK with at least one child aged ten and under were polled during the study, and all of the participants questioned confirmed that they were active users of the social networking website Facebook.

outside their trousers. A recent poll of fathers in Norway[3] revealed that many were struggling to strike a balance between work and home, feeling the pressure to excel in both areas. The researcher wrote that: 'They struggled with the Superman image. They feel they are now expected to give 110 per cent both at work and at home, and sometimes end up feeling that they don't give enough time to either.'

Being a parent is one of the most important and challenging roles that we can have and deserves our very best efforts. But we

3 Net Mums survey Jan 2011 Read more: http://www.dailymail.co.uk/femail/article-2536605/Shouldnt-call-Babybook-Two-thirds-parents-ONLY-post-Facebook-children-block-so.html#ixzz3NbDxIo18

need to dispel once and for all the myth of Supermum. And if we can acknowledge that parenting is not a spectator sport, it means that we can be free of the pressure to perform.

Let's lay down the comparisons, be real about both the joys and the challenges, decide how we want to parent in our particular family situation – and then simply do our best. We have nothing to prove. There really is no pressure to be a Superhero.

Superhero parents...

- ✓ Always have all the stuff for a morning of junk modelling
- ✓ Always return library books several days early
- ✓ Always redeem supermarket coupons before the expiry date
- ✓ Always know the school holiday dates
- ✓ Always get to the bottom of the ironing basket
- ✓ Always wash PE kit every Friday night
- ✓ Always co-ordinate lifts for their children and their friends for lots of extra curricular activities
- ✓ Always provide beautiful homemade cupcakes for the school bazaar
- ✓ Never double book for Parents evening and …
- ✓ Are never, ever late on the school run!

LAY DOWN THE GUILT

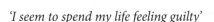

'I seem to spend my life feeling guilty'

I have had the privilege of speaking with thousands of parents over the years – they have shared with me their joys, fears, hopes and aspirations for their children. But time and time again they confide this: they feel guilty.

These parents are not serial offenders, most haven't got dreadful skeletons lying in the cupboard under the stairs just behind the hoover. No, they are ordinary mums and dads who are *tired* – not so much of doing the main task of parenting but of being told they are rubbish at it. One mum put it like this: 'Every time I hear an expert give a "foolproof" way to deal with the kids, I find that mine are an exception to the rule!'

And the school gate can be a scary place for the mum or dad not up-to-date with the latest idea. Another mum explained: 'At times I worried I should have pushed him a bit more with his reading and then another mum told me that was the worst thing I could do, saying – "You'll kill their love of books!"' But this poor mum went on to say that it wasn't just reading – it was potty training, vitamins, exercise, whether to stay at home or go back to work, whether to enforce strict bedtimes or be laid back about rules, whether to bath with them or not even think of it …

all these things caused guilt. 'At times my head whirls with it all,' she concluded.

As I write, I am in the middle of a tour called 'Parentalk'. I love these events – they give me the chance to speak to thousands of parents in a live setting about some of the issues closest to my heart. One of my favourite parts is when we say at the beginning, 'We want to share a secret with you, when it comes to their own kids, there are no experts – the people who write the books, the ones who appear on television and those who give advice in the columns of the magazines – all of them

are just people trying to get their own kids through as best they can. So above all, have confidence in your own parenting.

Nobody knows your child like you – and nobody loves them like you. So listen to what we say, try it, but if it doesn't work, try something else. There is no one way to be a *perfect* parent – but there are a hundred ways to be a *great* parent.'

Nobody sums up this issue of guilt better than a mum who wrote in to Care for the Family:

> *Mother guilt is attached to the umbilical cord,*
> *but it stays with you for life.*
> *You feel guilty about what you do*
> *and guilty about what you don't do.*
> *Guilty when you leave them*
> *and guilty when you pick them up.*
> *Guilty about what they eat,*
> *what they don't eat*
> *and even what they might eat.*
> *The guilt gets you at night,*
> *on the train,*
> *standing in the school playground*
> *and especially when you've left them to have a break.*
> *Then it usually gets attached to your purse*
> *and leads you to a toyshop.*
> *What mothers need*
> *is a jury of twelve good mothers and true*
> *to stand up and say*
> *'Not guilty m'lud'.*

The time when I most needed to hear that 'not guilty' verdict was on a memorable trip to London when our children were

3, 5, 7 and 9. We had seen the sights, successfully negotiated the Underground, and at five o'clock on an October evening, just as it was beginning to go dark, arrived back at Wandsworth station where we had left the car. Our two eldest began to argue, Charlotte thought George had dog poo on his shoe and didn't want to sit next to him. We had had a busy day and I was anxious to get back and irritated with their bickering. I got into the passenger seat and uttered the immortal words 'If you can't behave you'll have to walk home.' The argument subsided; we got in the car and set off. We had been driving for about ten minutes when George (nine) said 'Where's Charlotte?'

I still remember the feeling of utter panic as I looked round and realised that she wasn't in the car. We had driven off without her. At just seven-and-a-half years old we had left her behind in the middle of London. The next thirty minutes felt the longest of my life. Everything seemed to happen in slow motion. We did a sudden u-turn across London rush hour traffic and headed back to the station to find she wasn't where we had left her! I remember jumping out of the car and blindly running up and down the roads searching for a sight of her blonde curls and red hoodie. After what seemed an eternity we found her – walking up and down the next street with no idea where she (or more importantly we) were. She had thought the car was facing *up* the road, and, miffed with her brother, had stormed off, thinking that we would pick her up. Unfortunately the car was facing in the opposite direction, I hadn't taken a roll call, and, assuming everyone was in the car, we had set off without her. I have made many mistakes as a mum but that was probably the one that even now overwhelms me with guilt whenever I think about it.

When we feel we have really messed up, the guilt can be hard to bear. Almost worse can be the guilt that we feel in comparing ourselves to 'perfect' parents. Occasionally you come across them. On the Parentalk tour we give some tips to any guilt-inducing parents who might be in the audience. These mums and dads encourage other parents to follow their example because they really do have three perfect children. They save their pocket money for study-guides, always do their homework before playing on the computer, and offer to help with the washing-up because 'You've had a hard day at work, Mum.' If that's you:

Advice for the parents of three perfect children

1. *Don't knock it – you're blessed*

2. *Keep it to yourselves – stop sending us those 'Farleigh Family Christmas News' missives*

and, most important of all ...

3. *Don't even think of having a fourth. You're not a perfect parent – you just got lucky!*

CHILDREN WILL BE AS DIFFERENT AS CHALK AND CHEESE

Children will be as different as chalk and cheese

In the weeks before our third child was born, I remember wondering which of the other two children he would be like – and then being surprised afterwards to discover that he was different again!

Our children are unique, and if we have more than one child, we may well discover that they are as different as chalk and cheese. And if we are the parent of just one child, we will also soon discover how different they are to their peers. One may be challenging, the other compliant, and others a whole range of temperaments in between.

The chairman and founder of Care for the Family, Rob Parsons, often speaks about the differences between his two children, Katie and Lloyd. Katie was their first, and she was a typical compliant child. Rob writes:

> *The first thing Katie did when she came into the world was to apologise to the midwife for being a little late. Dianne and I thought we were the perfect parents. We tutted to each other as we watched other toddlers having tantrums in the aisles of supermarkets. Sometimes, with hardly concealed glee, we pointed out to other parents where they might be going wrong with their offspring … And then Lloyd came into our lives. The parenting gurus tell us that if your first child is shy, careful and compliant your second will be different. Lloyd was desperate not to disappoint those experts.[4]*

{ 4 Rob Parsons, *The Sixty Minute Mother*, Hodder & Stoughton (London 2009) }

In contrast, Richard's and my first child was our most challenging. Boundaries, in his view, were to be tested at all costs, just to make sure they were really there. I used to look at other parents with children who agreed to wear their coats, kept the water in the bath, ate their broccoli and didn't kick their siblings, and I'd ask myself, 'Where have I gone wrong?'

The truth was, I hadn't. Children are born with different temperaments, and, try as we might, it is not our task as parents to change them. Of course, I wanted to teach our son to have good qualities, such as being kind and thinking of others, but it is his challenging disposition that has enabled him to grow into a fun-loving, bright young man who lights up a room, isn't afraid to challenge the *status quo*, and has a heart for justice. (And now he even eats broccoli!)

Another of our boys was born with a fiercely competitive spirit, which can make even a game of tiddlywinks a challenge. 'Losing' in his mind 'is for losers'. In the early days I tried to change this trait in him. If his team lost at football I would remind him that it was only a game. But my words seemed to fall on deaf ears. I have come now to understand that winning is always going to be important to him. It's the way he is wired. Of course I wanted to teach him to lose (and to win) graciously. Losing a game of tennis to his older brother would invariably result in an outburst to rival John McEnroe, so we would try to encourage him to remain calm and to congratulate his opponent at the end of the match – even if it was between gritted teeth. Similarly, when the score has been in his favour we have suggested he tones down the victory lap around the court. It will be an area he will need to work on for the rest of his life, but if channelled well, that competitive edge is what will give him the focus and determination to persevere and succeed in life.

But it's not just a difference in personalities that many parents mention to me but so often a difference in the sexes. Our first child was a boy, the second a girl, and there shouldn't be any surprises that they were different! Having said that, the first time I changed my daughter's nappy I remember being

surprised that the wee arrived in a neat little puddle rather than a vertical jet stream that hit the ceiling and anyone else in range.

Now we have to be a bit careful here. If you happen to have children of both sexes it's not long before you realise that whoever wrote that little boys are made of 'slugs and snails and puppy-dogs' tails' and little girls of 'sugar and spice and all things nice' clearly never had kids.

It always used to irritate me that manufacturers put pink pockets on girls' jeans, so I couldn't pass them on to my boys. Gender stereotyping starts young on the high street. There are sparkly shoes for little princesses and commando shorts for little heroes.

And it's hard to beat. A friend of mine was determined not to give her children gender stereotypical toys. She gave up when the boys used the doll's pram as a go-cart and bit their sandwiches into the shape of guns, whereas her daughter became obsessed with glitter. These are generalisations of course, children are individuals and don't conform – some boys love playing with dolls, and some girls love being in the middle of the scrum with the roughest of the boys.

But, without falling into the trap of stereotyping, it might be worth remembering that, in at least some ways, boys and girl develop differently – and not just in the ability to wee in a straight line. Whilst some of the gender stereotyped behaviour is learned, experts agree that the differences between boys and girls go deeper, they are down to something more than upbringing.[5] Even in the womb, boys' and girls' brains are developing differently. Studies of early brain development show

5 Sheri Berenbaum, professor of psychology and pediatrics at Pennsylvania State University, as quoted in Woolston, Chris. Brain Development: Is the difference between boys and girls all in their heads? http://www.babycenter.com/0_brain-development-is-the-difference-between-boys-and-girls-a_10310673.bc.

that boys' brains have much more testosterone than girls'.[6] Once girls and boys are born, their brains continue to take different paths. MRI scans show that different areas in boys' and girls' brains grow at different rates, but eventually, they catch up with each other.

It was interesting watching the way my children of different sexes seemed to have different ways of playing and making friends. One day, on holiday at the beach, our children began happily paddling in a nearby stream. They were soon joined by two other children and played with them until lunchtime, building dams and constructing a system of waterworks that would have made the Department of the Environment proud.

When Charlotte, our daughter, returned to where we were sitting she told us all about her new best friend, Lucy. Lucy lived in London, she had two brothers, a new kitten, a hamster, a goldfish, a pink bedroom and a new butterfly hair clip. Her class teacher next term would be Mrs Webster. They were friends forever.

George, our son, returned a few minutes later. As no information from him was forthcoming, I enquired about the new friend he'd been digging alongside for the past few hours. He looked puzzled, paused for a moment and then said,

'Oh him … he's just a boy.'

For the boys, activity had been the centre of their relationship; they were perfectly happy digging together and not engaging in any conversation. In contrast, the girls had earnestly exchanged the minutiae of life in both their families.

I remember commenting to my husband that whereas Charlotte followed me all around the house chatting constantly

{ 6 *Margaret M. McCarthy, Professor of physiology at the University of Maryland* }

– it was a hard to get so much as a syllable out of one of our sons. Richard grunted and said,

> *'Mmm.'*

Exactly!

Whether or not they fit the stereotypes, and even if we have children of the same sex, it is likely they will be as different as chalk and cheese. But chalk and cheese have unique qualities, and one is not 'better' than the other. Writing on a blackboard with a piece of Stilton, or sprinkling grated chalk on top of spaghetti bolognese won't get you far. So let's not try to make our children someone they are not and cannot be. Let's celebrate the differences in their temperaments, look for the positives, and encourage the unique qualities that, in later life, will enable them to make a difference in the world.

Let's be the wind behind them and encourage them to be the boys and girls – in fact the *people* – that they were made to be.

DON'T LOOK SIDEWAYS

The first time I ventured out solo in my parents' car, after having passed my driving test, I had been driving for about ten minutes when I came to a narrow stretch of road between two parked cars. Having not been blessed with a sense of spatial awareness, I had no idea if I could fit through. A queue of traffic soon built up behind as I inched forward, causing all the A-type personality commuters, whose sorry fate it was to be behind me, a dangerous rise in blood pressure. Sweating profusely, I inched forward with no idea how I was going to negotiate that gap. I had read *The Highway Code* from cover to cover, but I could not remember it giving any advice or guidance for this situation.

As I veered terrifyingly close to the parked cars, the passenger door came within an inch of its life. The driver in the car behind me could contain herself no longer and jumped out to come to my rescue. She stood in front of my car and began walking backwards, gesticulating madly. 'Eyes straight ahead,' she shouted. 'Don't look sideways, look at me!' This woman was my saviour. As I focused ahead rather than on the parked cars to the sides, I found I could drive safely through the gap – without inflicting any scrapes or marks on my parents' car or the two cars on either side.

I later reflected that not only was this an excellent lesson about driving, but also for life itself. As a parent, I so often gave in to the temptation to take my eye off the destination and to look sideways – to make a comparison. It only resulted in feelings of discouragement in the belief that others were doing a better job than me.

The two hours between 10am and 12 noon on a Sunday were when these thoughts would be uppermost in my mind. We would go to the family service at our local church and invariably found ourselves sitting behind Mrs M and her three beautifully behaved children. Keeping our four under control often felt more like refereeing a wrestling match than engaging in morning worship. The antics in our row were in sharp contrast to the goings-on in front, where the family M children, with shiny shoes and blonde pigtails, would sit quietly and give the appearance of listening attentively throughout. Hardly a week would go by without Mrs M turning around to smile and say what became familiar words, 'Goodness! You've got your hands full.'

No doubt she meant well, but the comment did nothing to encourage us in our ability to parent with confidence. While centile charts are useful for monitoring our children's growth and development, and comparethemarket.com may help us land the best deal for car or travel insurance, comparison is not a good tool to keep in the toolbox of parenting.

One mum put it like this: 'It's so easy to look sideways and feel that everybody else is doing a much better job than you, and then to feel bad. When other peoples' children come to visit they are so polite – and I am genuinely surprised when other parents tell me that mine are too – when they visit them. I spend half my life hoping my kids won't give the game away about what I'm really like as a mother – but actually I'm giving it my best shot and my kids are fine.'

There is certainly always much we can learn as parents, and it's good to share stories and experiences and to encourage

others who are at the same life stage. The ancient book of Proverbs gives good advice,

> *Let your eyes look directly forward,*
> *and your gaze be straight before you.*
> *Ponder the path of your feet;*
> *then all your ways will be sure.*[7]

That advice got me through my driving career without too many scrapes, and it can protect the bodywork of parents too.

And remember the ghost in the machine: there is only one thing more annoying that seeing perfect parents with perfect kids and that's seeing what appear to be parents who have broken every rule in the book with kids who could have tea with the Queen without embarrassment. (Don't get me started!)

{ 7 Proverbs 4: 25, 26 (ESV) }

ASK YOURSELF: WHAT DOES A GOOD JOB REALLY LOOK LIKE

*Ask yourself: What does a good job **really** look like?*

One interesting thing about having four children is that, looking back, I can see how my attitudes have changed so much with each one. With our first, I would hardly let my husband, Richard, do a thing. I was the mother – and mothers know best.

This came to a head one evening at bedtime. Getting four children upstairs, bathed and with pyjamas on, teeth cleaned, stories read and into bed required the strategic know-how and planning of a military operation. Richard would always try to be home in time for stories, but the initial supervision of the bedtime routine usually fell to me. Maybe it was because I had been with the children all day, but by 7pm I just wanted to get them settled and into bed – no high-jinx or other antics – and I had the routine down to a fine art. Richard would arrive half way through the proceedings. Fun and games with his children was a highlight after a work-weary day – and he would invariably have fun and games galore up his sleeve, which usually involved lots of shrieking and running around or bouncing on beds. My attempts to get the children into bed quickly would be hijacked. My irritation at his casual approach to the bedtime routine would often focus on the lack of supervision given to teeth cleaning. The children would all clean their teeth – but not in the way that I thought it should be done. Richard simply did not seem able to grasp the required amount of horizontal and vertical brushes that are needed to instruct a six-year-old in dental hygiene. 'Just give them a good doing son' was simply not enough! And, on more than one occasion, I found myself taking over. But the honest truth is that I was going over the top. By the time our fourth came along I would hardly worry if the poor soul was soaking his dentures in the bath.

Richard and I have parented in different ways and I have often had to moderate my natural tendency to want to be in control. I've had to make a supreme effort to bite my tongue.

At some point I remembered a question that I sometimes asked in workplace appraisals: 'What does a good job look like?' A 'good' job can mean very different things to different people. In hindsight I am sure Richard's toothbrushing supervision was more than adequate (all four still have their teeth as young adults!) but my inner belief that only my way was best, often led to Richard backing off.

If you are a mum parenting with a dad, try to back off a little and allow dad to be involved. And dads, find ways to engage with the routine jobs – meal times, bedtimes, the school run – as well as the fun and games (important as that is). Of course we see some situations when couples break up shortly after the birth of a child. In these circumstances it can be difficult, but if at all possible, keeping both parents involved can be of enormous benefit to the child.

If you are parenting alone, take all the help you can get, including accepting support from grandparents, other family members, neighbours and friends. And if they aren't doing the job exactly as you would, before jumping in to set them right, press the pause button and ask yourself, 'What does a good job *really* look like?'

"Right daddy, off you go to bed first so there's no silly business, ok?"

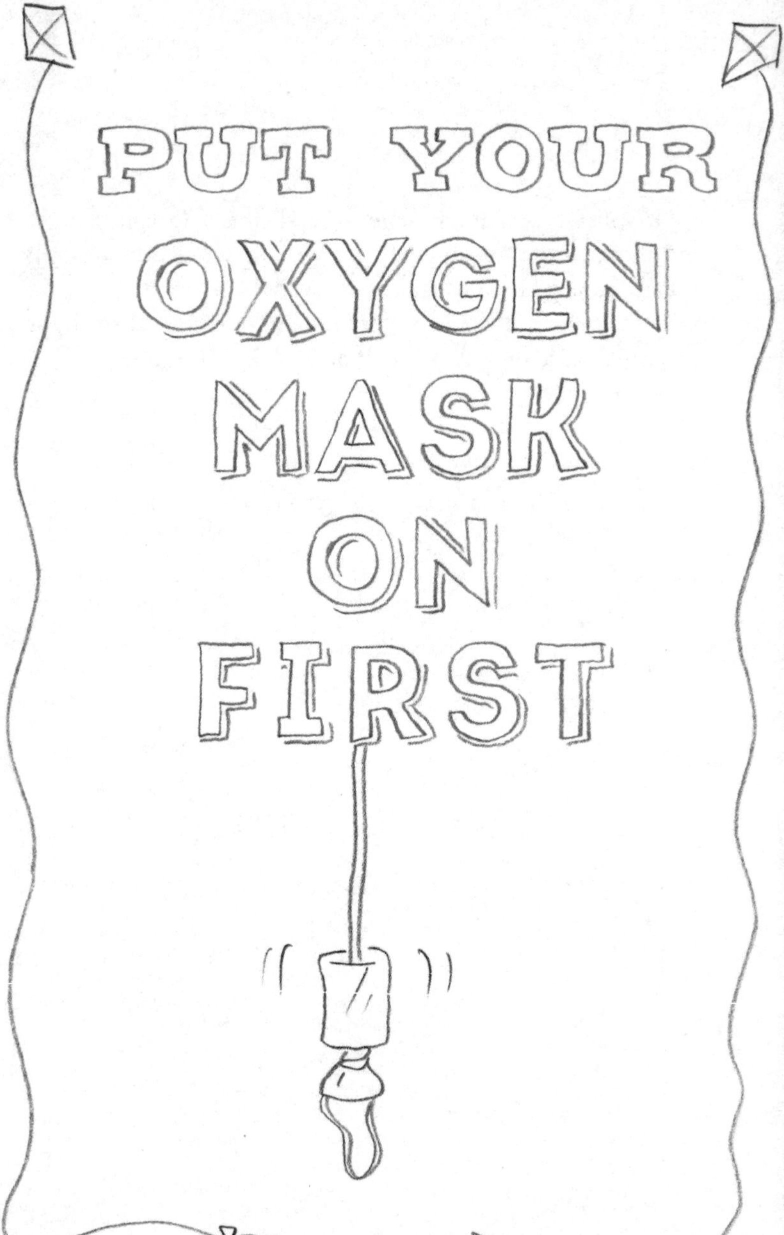
PUT YOUR
OXYGEN
MASK
ON
FIRST

Put your oxygen mask on first

We'll all be familiar with the aircraft safety announcement telling people to ensure they put their own oxygen masks on first before attending to their children. This direction may sound counter-intuitive for parents as we seem programmed to care for our children at all costs. But attending to our own needs first in an emergency on a plane means we have the air we need in order to help, support and care for our children in the most effective way possible.

As parents, our heartfelt desire to do the very best for our children can be all-consuming. If we are not careful, the result of pouring ourselves totally into our children can be that we neglect to look after ourselves or fail to make time to invest in important adult relationships in our lives.

The term when our youngest started school and our oldest was in year 6, Richard suggested that we asked a grandparent or friend to come to stay so that we could go away for a weekend, just the two of us. His observation was that we had got into a rut of only ever talking about the children or issues related to them. He wanted a weekend away when, just for a moment, we could forget the relentlessness of family responsibilities, and walk, laugh and have fun together, like we used to BC. He had a voucher for a hotel in Wales set in a beautiful valley surrounded by rolling hills. The restaurant promised delicious, locally sourced produce that put our routine family suppers of sausages, fish fingers or pasta into the shade. It sounded such a lovely idea.

But to Richard's disappointment, I said 'No'. My reluctance

was rooted in the fact that I felt we would, in some way, be letting our children down by leaving them behind for 24 hours.

In hindsight I realise how wrong I was. For Richard and I, the demands of four children, particularly when they were young, were so draining that we found we were only giving each other the dregs of our time at the end of the day. We had long to-do lists in the evening: homework to be supervised, spellings to be learnt, lifts to be given, a meal to be prepared, football kits to be washed, children to be bathed, stories to be read, and bedtime to be negotiated. The mantra we adopted – 'divide and conquer' – worked well. We would decide who was going to be responsible for which task and set about doing them in parallel – Richard would be in one part of the house, working through his list and I would be in another. But while that may work for getting through all the evening chores before midnight, it is not a good habit to adopt long term. If you are parenting together, avoid slipping into 'parallel living' by looking out for opportunities for things you can do *together*.

Fortunately, sense later prevailed, and we did eventually enjoy a night away on our own. It was one of the best investments of our time that we ever made. I realised at this time that it was important that we made time for each other – not just in things like an occasional night away – which is not always possible but in small ways. It always involved a little planning and the help of others but to us it became a lifeline.

Soon after, some wise friends encouraged us to put a 'date night' into the diary each week, so we did. This date doesn't have to be complicated or even cost money – our first 'outing' on our own was to go out for a drink together at our local pub, although some more imaginative ones followed, including a closely fought game of crazy golf (Richard won... but only just!).

It's simply a time away from the usual demands to focus on each other, have fun and talk – in fact, to put on that oxygen mask for the week ahead.

One of the advantages of the primary years is that (I hope) you have some hours of evening left after the children are in bed. Make the most of it – the teenage years when they are up and about all evening will be here before you know it! To save on getting a babysitter we have had many date nights 'at home', no checking of e-mails, folding of washing, DIY jobs or other household chores allowed but simply time together. Sometimes we lit a candle and cooked a nice meal, we watched a film or simply chatted over a glass of wine. When we have had a babysitter we have gone to the cinema, out for a drink or a pizza, or in the summer for a walk and a picnic. For a number of years when I was at home and Richard was at work we seized a 'date night' moment during

the day, and would grab a coffee together at lunchtime whilst the children were at school. Find the time that works best for you – it will involve being both flexible and creative.

It has been well said that, 'The best thing a father can do for his children is to love their mother' and of course that works for loving fathers as well. There are obviously other reasons for investing in our couple relationship – but the fact that it benefits our children is not a bad place to start. For many it is not easy but, if you possibly can, think about booking a babysitter and going on a marriage course – a kind of MOT for your relationship. We went on one when our children were in the primary years and it was one of the best investments we could have made.

If you are parenting on your own it's equally important to give time to adult relationships that energise you. Through Care for the Family, I meet a lot of single parent mums and dads. Many feel isolated and alone, and anything we can do to ease that burden can be life changing. One Mum spoke of the difficulties she faced:

Twenty-four-hour parenting – there's no one else when you've just had enough. Even ordinary things can seem like mountains to climb. I'm scared of getting flu because somebody has to care for my kids. The other day I had to go into hospital for a minor operation but first I had to get somebody to have my two children for a couple of days. You'd think it would be easy but sometimes it seems impossible. As for money – it's often hand to mouth. I work outside the home part-time but even so we don't have much fun. I don't care so much about myself but I want them to have what other kids have.

There's just nobody to talk to, nobody to say, 'Don't be daft' or 'Let the baby cry for a while' or 'You're doing a great job'. I so often have the sense that I really am on my own[8]

My heart especially goes out to this single parent at that last comment, 'There's just nobody to talk to.' I know it's not always possible but if we can find others to share with, it will make a massive difference. And perhaps those of us who have friends who are single parents can try to go the second mile to be there for them.

Jill, a single mum with two young children, said, 'My other adult friends have been a lifeline to me. We arrange to meet up a couple of times a month, either for a coffee during the day or sometimes for a drink in the evening. I have to fight for the time, but it's worth it. I've discovered I'm a much better mum to my kids when I've had some adult company. It helps me keep a sense of perspective and stops everything getting on top of me.'

Finding time to keep our own relationships strong – no matter how we do it – is vital – not just for our sake but for our kids sake. The oxygen mask will drop down from a panel above your seat – remember to put it on first and everyone will benefit.

{ 8 Rob Parsons The Sixty Minute Mother, Page 66 }

LISTENING
SAYS
YOU
MATTER

Listening says 'You matter'

I was recently invited to a networking event for women. I was pleased to have received the invitation as there was a particular guest that I was keen to meet. I had admired her for some time, and felt sure I would have lots to learn from her experience. I arrived and made my way into the room, which was already full. The organiser greeted me and introduced me to a group of people, which included the person I was keen to connect with. I couldn't believe my good fortune. We began talking, but before too long I became aware that her attention was not on me, but on a conversation going on just behind my left shoulder. I battled on for a few minutes – and then stepped aside so she could join the other group. Her distraction and failure to listen made me feel insignificant and invisible, and I soon made my apologies and left the gathering. However many pearls of wisdom she may have shared with me at a later time, her inability to listen and to engage with me rendered them worthless.

This was in sharp contrast to a friend I called on in a moment of need some months ago. Looking back, I realise that it wasn't a great time to have just dropped in on her, unannounced. Her husband was self-employed, and they were up to their eyes trying to get his paperwork in order. But somehow she sensed my need. She pushed the spreadsheets to one side, put the kettle on, turned off her phone, looked directly into my eyes and simply said, 'Tell me about it.' And I did. I will always remember the feeling of worth and value that she gave me when she sat at the table with me and let me talk.

As parents we have the same power at our disposal. We can make our children feel valued and special, we can let them understand that they are the most important people in our lives, and we can give them the belief that they matter just by listening. Henry, aged five, loved animals, and when he grew up he wanted to be a vet. I remember him saying to me one day, 'I think my hamster is having babies.'

It was seven o'clock in the evening and I had been in my new part-time job for exactly two days and was trying to read an office 'How we do things' manual that made *War and Peace* look like a pamphlet. I ignored him.

I felt reasonably justified in this for two reasons: firstly, the said hamster had been alone in the cage for as long as we had owned it; secondly 'Spike' was male. So if Spike had somehow managed this feat, then both Henry and I were going to make a lot of money.

I didn't take my eyes off 'Employees' responsibilities on noticing breaches of IT procedures' and said, 'Not now darling – later.'

Usually children are content with the 'We'll do it later' routine – they believe us and we believe ourselves as we are saying it. But sometimes 'later' is not good enough. When I saw his face I knew that this was one of those moments.

This was a *now* moment.

We can't always do it – we probably shouldn't always do it – but the truth is that so often it doesn't take much time to make

a child feel not only listened to – but special. On this occasion
– although alas, not on every one – I chose well. I laid down the
manual and heard myself say, 'Well darling, that is amazing –
now where is that book on hamsters we bought?'

Another time, our daughter Charlotte, who was about five,
had just returned from a friend's house, where they had seen
a very exciting film with a convoluted plot. It involved an ice
queen and an enchanted wood, a hummingbird, a knight and
a castle, and a lengthy cast list besides. We were sitting around
the kitchen table, and she began to tell us the story, describing

everything, almost frame by frame, in minute detail. As the plot unravelled, I found my mind wandering – I think my eyes fell on a magazine on the table beside me – an article, something about decluttering your home. She continued for a while without missing a beat, and then stopped mid-sentence and said to me,

'Mummy, you aren't listening.'

'Yes, I am darling,' I replied, still wondering at the complete absence of piles of papers and the neatly stacked jumpers on shelves in the glossy pictures of a minimalist home …

'No, you're not, Mummy. You need to listen with your eyes!'

And she was right – my wandering gaze had led me to disengage with the exploits of the ice queen and the hummingbird some minutes before.

When our children are small, kneeling down, perhaps cupping their face in our hands and giving them eye contact as they describe their drawing of the cat or the model dinosaur they made out of junk conveys to them that we are interested in them, that they are important to us[9].

The challenge is that we see the world through adult eyes. The things we think are important are often not so high on our children's agenda. Listening with our ears and our eyes generally means stopping what we are doing – finishing that email, checking that text, chopping that onion, or emptying the dishwasher – and saying to them, 'You matter.'

9 Singh, SK. 'Family Communication' *Global Journal of Arts and Management, pp* 11-13 (2011).

IT'S GOOD TO TALK

Our son had just moved up to junior school, and it was about three weeks into term. He arrived in our bedroom in his pyjamas one Tuesday morning to say he wasn't well – he had been sick – and so wouldn't be able to go to school. He took me to the bathroom to show me the evidence, and sure enough the loo was full of what looked decidedly like vomit. However I couldn't help but feel unsure of the truth of the story as this child looked the picture of health. My suspicions were confirmed when I went downstairs for breakfast and found a newly opened packet of muesli. Shreddies or Rice Krispies were the cereals of choice. He didn't like nuts and made a huge fuss if there was a raisin in his bowl – I knew he wouldn't have touched muesli. Sherlock Holmes famously said to Dr Watson, 'Watson, you see, but you don't observe.' I saw, but unlike Watson I also observed. And the penny dropped. Muesli, masquerading as sick, had been jettisoned down the loo. In fact, so convincing was it, that son number one had been within an inch of pulling the wool over his mother's eyes and securing a day off school. I was singularly unimpressed and particularly cross with him for lying. We were already late, so after telling him off, I packed him off to school with his tail between his legs.

It was only later that evening that I took the time to allow him to talk and the whole story came tumbling out. Sometimes our children are just being naughty, but on this occasion I realised that my son had been trying to tell me something – and I hadn't really been listening. Tuesday was swimming day, and he had been put in a swimming class that was too difficult for him. He had been so anxious about it that he had staged the muesli episode so he wouldn't have to go. Having discovered the truth, I was able to see the swimming teacher who arranged for him to be moved to a lower class the following week.

Life is busy and it is not always possible, but looking back I could have saved that child a great deal of angst and heartache if only I had only spotted the cues he was giving me. They may not be ready to or even want to share their hearts with us, but at least we can give them the opportunity. Try allowing a moment – in the car, at bedtime, after a meal – just to allow time to talk.

One mum told me of the time her six-year-old told her about a boy who was bullying him. She said that Tom had been in a low key for weeks and she was thinking of taking him to the doctor, but one evening as they were playing a board game together it all came pouring out: 'Mummy, Sam,

one of the big boys, says that I've got a disease and I'll be dead by Monday.' Claire remembers thinking, 'And so it begins – not seven years old and it has started.' Claire was bullied herself as a child, not just in primary school, but throughout her teenage years, and it had affected her badly. She had had little help from her parents – she remembers her mother saying, 'Oh it's just words – say something worse back.' But her mother didn't understand what it was like, to wake with the sick feeling in your stomach and dread school – sometimes just because of only one child. She wanted to do better for Tom. My friend said that she talked it over with her partner that evening and the next day chatted with a close friend who also had a child at that school. She decided to speak to a school counsellor about it in confidence. She said the counsellor was brilliant. She mentioned to Claire that a bullied child faces a dilemma: 'I need to tell my parents but if I do they may "go up the school" and make it worse'. They know they have

to go on living with the bully after we have done our parental bit. Claire said that she never really did discover what went on in the background, but over the following weeks it seemed that either the boy who was doing the bullying had been spoken to or he had chosen to move on to somebody else. But one of the most telling things the counsellor said to Claire stayed with her long after the incident had passed: 'Keep listening to him. Let him know he can always come to you – and you will take him seriously.' Claire and I were having coffee months later when she said to me, 'As I look back on it I feel quite moved and a bit sad at how long he endured it all without saying a thing. And it struck me the other day – if we hadn't been playing Ludo together that evening he might never have told me'. And as she did, the image of half a packet of muesli down the loo flashed across my mind!

Those 'muesli moments' occur in all our lives – those times when we are scared or worried or confused. As adults, we often learn to hide them but, especially with children, it's important that we give them the *time* to talk them out.

LOVE THEM AND LET THEM KNOW

Rockleaze Rangers football club provided the opportunity for a release of pent up energy for our three boys and their friends, and a freezing ninety minutes on the sideline for us parents, every Saturday morning during the football season. This club was wonderfully well run by volunteer dads, who were our heroes. The time, energy and organisation that they invested in the club were set to rival any Premier League manager. Fitness was encouraged, team formations were planned, league games completed and tournaments played against rival clubs. The focus of the year, however, was the end of season Award Ceremony in the school hall. Coca-Cola and crisps, with awards and trophies for every achievement imaginable – most improved player, best goal scored, best goal saved, best tackle made, to name but a few. Whilst each child received an award, the biggest trophy that every boy dreamed of winning was 'Player of the Year'. Ed had played well that year, he had made it to the first team and scored the winning goal in the tournament – we knew he was in with a good chance. The only other contender was his friend Alfie, but Alfie had won Player of the Year the year before and hadn't scored the winning goal – so we were pretty confident Ed would be walking home with the trophy held high that evening. As the evening drew to a climax, the tension mounted. Ed was in the front row with his mates, who were as confident as he was of his achievement. The manager stepped forward and make the announcement: Player of the Year would go to … not Ed Hill or even Alfie Harris, but to … Dan Smith, a complete outsider.

Whilst our task that night was to console a disappointed eight-year-old, there was also the opportunity to teach him an important life lesson. The world gives our children the message that they are loved and accepted when they are successful and do well. But as parents, we have the opportunity to give them a rather different message. Whether or not they come top in the spelling test, are picked for the netball team, get a good part in the play, or even win Rockleaze Rangers' Player of the Year award, we have the opportunity to show them that our love for them isn't based on what they achieve, but on who they are. The most precious gift we can give our children is the knowledge that they are loved *anyway*.

It's as if each child has an emotional tank inside them that is crying out to be filled with love. Just as the petrol gauge on the car shows how much fuel is in the tank, our children's behaviour is often the gauge that shows us how full their 'emotional tank' is – how loved they feel.

Even on a bad day, most of us parents know that we love our children. The question to ask ourselves, though, is whether we are showing them that love in a way that they can understand, a way that really connects with them. Are we filling up their tank so that they *know* they are loved.

In his book *The 5 Love Languages*,[10] Gary Chapman gives some insight into this. He says that there are five different ways

10 Gary Chapman, *The Five Love Languages: How to Express Heartfelt Commitment to Your Mate* Northfield Publishing 1995; Moody Press 2015. Chapman describes how he had begun to see a pattern after twelve years of counselling couples who felt that their spouses didn't love them. When he asked them how they wanted their spouses to show them love, their answers fell into the five categories he eventually called the five love languages. http://www.5lovelanguages.com/faqs/love-languages/

that we can show someone that we love them – what he calls the five 'love languages'. These love languages are: words, time, actions, gifts and touch.

For each of our children (and for each one of us), one or two of these ways will be more important than the others: this is the love language, or the *way* of communicating love, that really connects with them. This means that if we can work out which of these ways will connect best with our child and learn to use it, then we will be saying 'I love you' in a way that they really can hear, in a language they understand and we will be filling their emotional tank.

The truth is, children need all these expressions of love, but as they get older we can begin to work out which of these ways is most meaningful for them. We then have a powerful tool at our disposal. There is no greater gift we can give our children than for them to grow up knowing that we love them and that we do so regardless of their looks, their successes or their failures … we love them *anyway*. In the next five chapters we are going to take a look at each of those 'love languages' in turn.

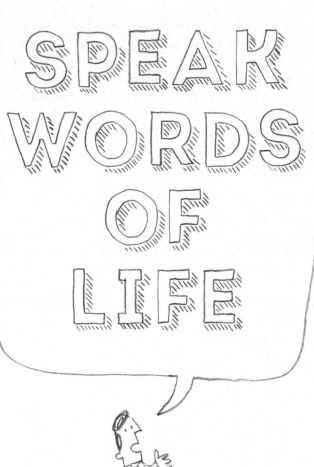

♡ love language 1

Speak words of life

♡

Much of the ancient book of Proverbs contains bite-sized wisdom about the way we use our words. One of the most memorable reminds us: 'The tongue has the power of life and death.'[11] They are strong words indeed, but they do point out the sheer power of the words we speak.

In the early years, it is relatively easy to say encouraging and affirming words to our children. Our son learns to recognise the first letter of his name, or we catch our daughter sharing her toys, and we readily heap on praise and affirmation, telling them how clever or kind or generous they are.

However, as time goes on and our children move into the primary years, I have found it easy to slip into focusing on the negatives – nagging and pointing out what is wrong rather than spotting what is right and praising them for it

Some time ago, our youngest asked if he could wash the car. We gave him the equipment, and he made a reasonable job of it. However, armed with a hose and some free time he found lots of other things that he believed could do with dousing – including his brother! A water fight soon ensued and I told him off in no uncertain terms for the tsunami he'd created. It was only later that I realised that I'd had nothing to say about the sparkling clean car – least of all making a point of praising him for it.

For one of our children, words of praise or encouragement are especially important. When he was about 11 years old, I was looking for something in his bedroom and discovered a

{ 11 Proverbs 18:21 }

shoebox under his bed. I took the lid off and found it was full of cards, notes and scraps of paper. They were all addressed to him and had kind and encouraging words on them; over the years he had saved them. In the evening I asked him about it and he said, 'It's my treasure box. If I'm feeling sad I take it out and read the words people have said, and it makes me feel good.'

I remember meeting a dad at a Care for the Family event. He had four stepchildren, who divided their time between two homes; they spent half the week with him and the rest of the time with their biological dad. He told me about a special wall they had in their kitchen. They called it the 'sticker wall' because they stuck all kinds of things that they could be proud of on it. He said the children weren't top of the class at school, nor were they just great at sport. Nevertheless, all kinds of different achievements were celebrated – achievements that were special just for that family. And it wasn't just the children's achievements that were celebrated. One sticker read, 'You did really good driving today Dad' and another, 'Mummy is the best brownie maker in the world'. When visitors came to the house, the children would grab them by the hand and drag them through to the kitchen to see the wall. He told me that he would watch their hearts swell with pride as visitors admired all the stickers.

There are so many different ways to give encouragement to our children. As well as recognising their successes and achievements, perhaps we can a give a word of praise to recognise our daughter's character and effort. Or we could write a note of encouragement on the banana in our son's lunch box saying, 'You'll be great on the team today – go you!' One family we know has a birthday tradition. After the candles have been blown out on the cake, they go round the table and each member of the family says something that they love or admire about the birthday girl or boy that they can take with them into the year ahead. Words not just for birthdays, but for life!

♡ love language 2

*It's quality **and** quantity time*

♡

For a number of years I swallowed the mantra that it is quality time, not quantity time, that is important. But the sobering truth is that although we can't always give our children quantity time, they need both. So often it's the amount of time we spend with them that lays the foundation for our relationship and allows our quality time together to flourish. Author Gretchen Rubin said of our children's lives 'The days are long, but the years are short' and now that I am standing on the threshold of our children leaving home I know how true that is.

Our youngest, Henry, used to jump into our bed every single morning, and a little ritual developed. As Henry snuggled in Richard would get up and have a shower, then come back into the bedroom and throw his wet towel on top of Henry's head. Henry would laugh and giggle and pull it off.

This went on for years, morning after morning, but then one morning as Richard got out of bed to have his shower we realised there was no Henry. He hadn't served notice on us that the game was over, and that he wasn't coming any more, but the fact was, that particular door on his childhood had now closed. However challenging family life can be, try not to wish their childhoods away.

With four children and lots going on in our lives at work and at home, we found that it was difficult to find time with each of our children individually – one-to-one time when we could give them focussed attention. We began a routine where one of us would take one of the children to Tesco for breakfast on a

Saturday morning. They would take it in turns and could decide which of us they wanted to take them.

All went well initially until I noticed that my husband increasingly became their companion of choice. Most of us are more insecure than we would like to admit and I began to wonder why they didn't want me to take them. Was I not a fun mummy? Further investigation uncovered the reason. While I had been insisting that they had a 'sensible' breakfast of cereal, orange juice and toast, I discovered that breaking all the rules, Richard was allowing them to enjoy chocolate eclairs, cheesy Wotsits and marshmallows, all washed down with a bottle of Coca-Cola! I decided to put my resolve to give them 'five a day' on hold just for that moment, as I reminded myself that the purpose of this outing was never was about the breakfast. It was simply about spending time together, and I needed to relax the rules if I was ever going to get a look in!

Generally, the conversation wouldn't be about anything significant, just time spent together. We would talk about football stickers, glitter pens or the latest playground craze, but just occasionally we would hear about something more significant. I remember one of our children, who had recently started school, confiding to me in hushed tones across the table that he didn't want to go the school the following week because he didn't know where to put his lunch box when he arrived. That one was fairly easily resolved. Others were more challenging. There were conversations about perceived injustices at school, struggles with friendships, or hopes and dreams that they had. Plans to play for Aston Villa, to be a fighter pilot, to own a mushroom restaurant called Fungi (… don't ask!) and to be a lead singer in a rock band were all dreamed up over breakfast at Tesco.

Making the most of the time we have with them – quality and quantity time – doesn't have to be complicated or expensive. It doesn't have to include deep communication, it is time spent just *being* – hanging out or simply engaging in the ordinary things of family life together. Things like making biscuits, going to the park, playing football or watching television – activities where our children know that they, rather than the activity, are the focus of our attention.

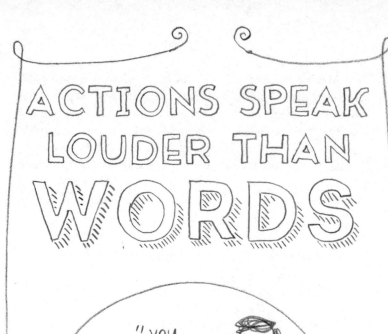

♡ love language 3

Actions speak louder than words

♡

There are days as parents when it seems as if we have enrolled in long-term service. The list of jobs we do for our children can feel monotonous and never-ending. When they are babies we feed them at hourly intervals, wind them, sooth them, rock them to sleep, change nappies and begin the process over again. The tasks in the primary years may be more varied but are equally relentless. Cooking meals, tidying toys, washing clothes, finding socks, reading stories, supervising bed time, making packed lunches, listening to them read, helping with homework, taking them to football, to Brownies, to ballet … and on it goes. We certainly don't want to become doormats, and we do our children no favours if we don't equip them to do things for themselves, but for some children our actions are particularly important: they convey to them that we love them. As they get older we can focus on doing things for them that they can't do themselves, or, for whatever reason, perhaps haven't time to do for themselves.

Things I have done for my children that I know have meant a lot to them include helping them to find school books which they have mislaid, giving them a lift when they could have walked, and making them a special packed lunch for a school trip. They are all jobs they could, and often do, do themselves, but just making the effort on those occasions to do it for them was a great way to say, 'I love you.'

♡ love language 4

Gifts are not just for birthdays

♡

Pester Power is the name of a popular booklet that Care for the Family produced with the Consumer Council to help parents navigate the challenges of bringing up children in our consumer-based materialistic society. Our children are growing up in a world where the media message is that they are what they own, their identity is in what they wear, and their values are aligned by the music they listen to. As parents, we need to be wise in the way we use our money. While we cannot 'buy' love, for some children gifts from parents are tangible evidence of their love and affection.

It is the thought behind the gift that conveys love and not the money involved. When I first spent a night away when speaking for Care for the Family, I bought some chocolate bars and put one on each of my children's beds. It became something of a tradition (though remembering to buy four Mars bars often felt like the last straw in the business of packing up to leave!).

While all of our children enjoyed the chocolate, for one of them gifts are particularly important and it signified much more. It said to her, 'I love you. I loved you enough to think of buying this for you, and when you enjoy it, you will be reminded again that you are loved.'

Small gifts can make a difference – a T-shirt when on holiday, a flower, a pencil or notebook from a gift shop, a rubber ball – all costing little in money but conveying love.

I was recently speaking at a summer conference and agreed to meet a young mum for coffee. Her daughter came over to join us. We hadn't met before, but she told me with much excitement that she had had just celebrated her eighth birthday, and had come to ask her mum for her £5 birthday money to spend. The money was duly handed over with the warning that after it was spent it was gone. Two minutes later she came skipping back across the hall and with a broad grin on her face presented me with an enormous bar of Cadbury's chocolate. I was overwhelmed at her generosity. No amount of convincing could persuade her to take it back. Alongside words, gifts are one of the ways I most feel loved, and in eight-year-old Hannah I had found a kindred spirit. And that simple gesture had given a big clue to her mum that, for Hannah, token gifts – not just on birthdays – would say to her 'I love you.'

♡ love language 5
PLEASE HOLD ME

An organisation that I work with in South Africa has a wonderful programme that provides support and care for the hundreds of vulnerable children in South Africa who have been orphaned as a result of HIV/Aids. The programme is called *Ngibambe* which means 'please hold me'. I met Graeme Schnell, the CEO, when he visited the UK recently, and he told a wonderful story. Graeme had been visiting one of the *Ngibambe* projects. As he walked across the schoolyard, one of the children came running towards him, tripped and fell. Instinctively, he scooped her up in his arms to comfort her. Seconds later he found himself mobbed by a crowd of orphans, all clamouring to be picked up and held. These children were hungry for the profound power of touch to convey love.

Although it may feel awkward to start with, most mums and dads don't need much teaching before they know how to cuddle a baby. And when our children are young we can take every opportunity to have a cuddle with them, to hold them – while watching the television, after they have taken a tumble, or when reading them a story or wrapping them in a soft, warm towel at bath time.

For one of our children, this is his primary love language. If he ever had a cut knee, was upset or worried, just giving him a cuddle would reassure him. The world would seem safe and he would feel loved. He is now six foot, three inches tall – and still occasionally needs a hug from his mum!

There are lots of opportunities to snuggle up with our children when they are young, but as they reach the end of the primary years it can begin to be less easy. Their need for a cuddle is no less great, but timing can be everything! One of our boys has never forgotten the moment that I gave him an enthusiastic kiss and hug at the school gate in full view of the Ist XV rugby team, who had just assembled on the coach. He still needed lots of hugs but the best place was in the hallway before we left the house! A hand on the shoulder when they are at the computer, rough and tumble play, or sitting close to them while watching TV are all opportunities to show them we love them through the power of touch.

One boy, who had just started secondary school, trying to balance 'looking cool' in front of his friends with the affection he still needed, put it like this, 'my parents don't hug me any more. But when no one's looking, I wish they still would.'

Touch – it's simple, but so powerful. We all need a lot of *Ngibambe*!

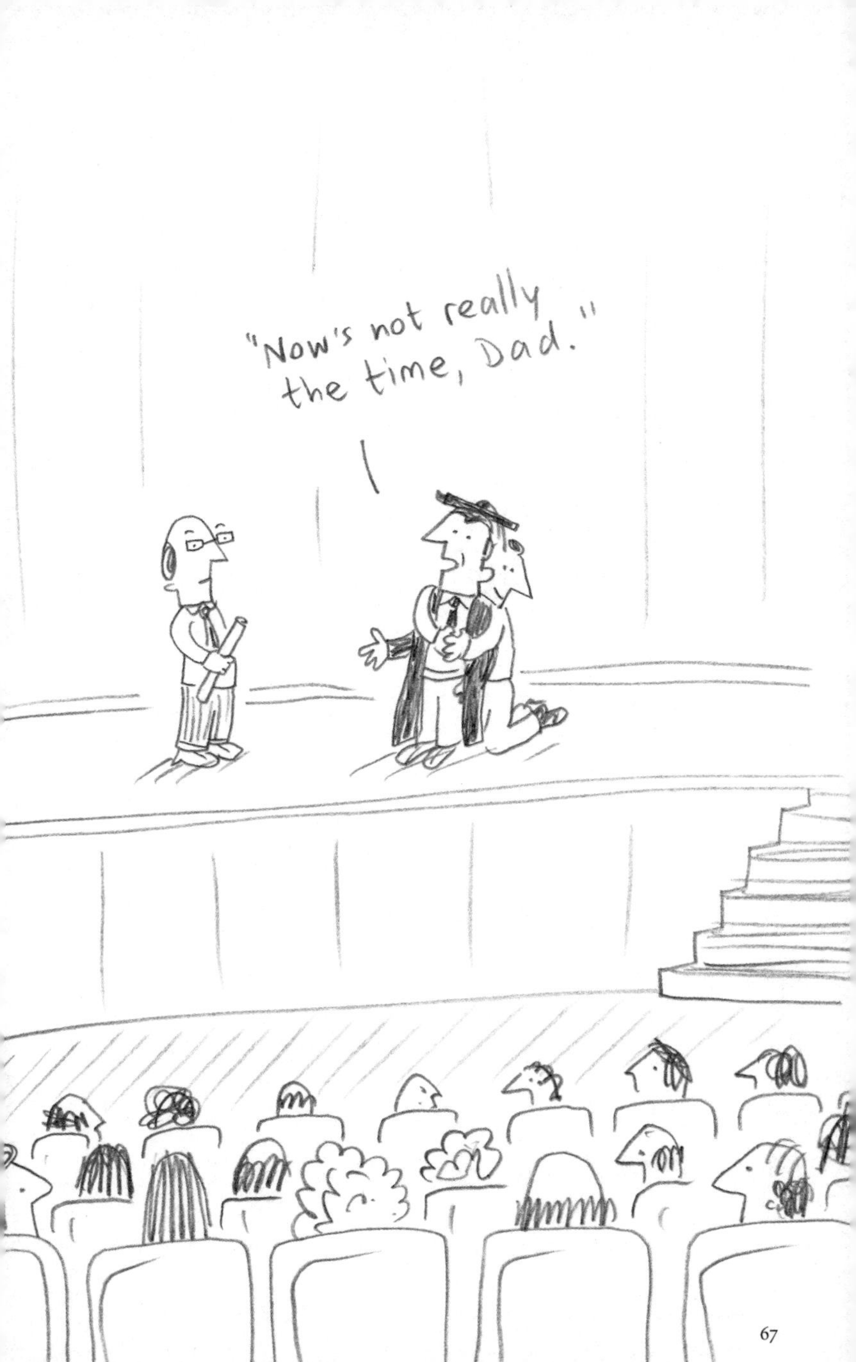
"Now's not really the time, Dad."

LAUGHTER IS THE BEST MEDICINE

Laughter is the best medicine

It was a normal Wednesday afternoon when my friend Cathy embarked on the afternoon school run. A busy evening of back-to-back activities lay ahead. She pulled up outside the school and sat in the car with her younger daughter waiting for the older one to appear. Without guile, her daughter, looked up and asked, 'Mummy, do you think you will be a better granny than you are a mummy?'

I too have experienced moments like that – moments when our child's unwitting comments seem to suck all the air from our lungs.

In a gracious reply, Cathy asked what her daughter meant and listed all the many things she did as her mum. The CV was impressive: providing a taxi service, cooking meals, helping with music practice and homework, washing, ironing, braiding hair … and so it went on.

When she finished, her daughter nodded. 'I know that,' she replied. 'It's just that we just don't seem to have much fun.' Cathy admitted to me when she told me the story that her daughter was right. Her family's busy schedule of activity meant there was little time for fun and laughter together.

The primary years can be some of the busiest and most challenging. Younger children in the family may have gifted us with the legacy of sleepless nights – add to that the physical exertion required to parent children in the daylight hours: driving them to ballet, swimming, football and drama classes, helping with homework and dealing with discipline – and it should be no surprise that sometimes a triple espresso or an energy drink is the only way we feel able to get through the day.

If we are working outside the home, this season often coincides with the very stage in our career when our work requires 110% of our focus and attention. For others, redundancy and unemployment leads to the intense pressure of seeking work and managing to make ends meet. Life can be hard. As well as all the ordinary things that are part of the deal of managing a home – kitchens to clean, meals to cook, shirts to iron, bills to pay – we may also have other challenges such as relationships under pressure, parenting alone, elderly parents to care for, illness or disability in the family, multiple births or children with additional needs. Somehow the relentlessness of life can take over and we go into survival mode.

The writer of the book of Proverbs wrote that 'A cheerful heart is good medicine'[12] and, 3,000 years later, science agrees. Laughter is good for us. Research shows that when we laugh, the tissue that lines our blood vessels expands. This increases blood flow and improves the health of our arteries. Researcher Michael Miller told *New Scientist* that a healthy lifestyle would include not only 30 minutes of exercise three times a week, but 15 minutes of hearty laughter each day.[13]

Press the pause button on the treadmill of activity and take time to laugh and have fun together. My husband is much better at this than me. I remember one 'sleep over' party (another misnomer!) for a large number of ten-year-old boys. No sleep had taken place and it was now the small hours of the morning. Not only was I tired but I was imagining the wrath of Mrs Bishop

12 Proverbs 17:22
13 *The Week* magazine, March 25, 2005; University of Maryland Medical Center. (2009) *Laughter is the Best Medicine for Your Heart.* http://umm.edu/news-and-events/news-releases/2009/laughter-is-the-best-medicine-for-your-heart.

descending on me the following morning when I returned her son Ned to her minus his obligatory eight hours sleep. My entreaties for the boys to quieten down had (unsurprisingly) fallen on deaf ears. Moreover Richard seemed to be ignoring the commotion and to add insult to injury had begun to snore. My exasperation boiled over and I woke him up and kicked him out of bed with a request to instil some discipline and some sleep to the occupants of George's bedroom. He obligingly turned the light on and set off down the corridor. However instead of a descending calm, the noise level increased by 100 decibels plus – armed with a giant Super Soaker water pistol he had crept into

the room through a trap door from the roof space and begun the biggest water fight imaginable. The shouts and screams could be heard for miles! The boys may not have had their quota of sleep – and Mrs Bishop was as cross, as I feared – but amidst much hilarity and laughter the boys enjoyed a party to remember! Let's not take ourselves too seriously.

Laughter can be about the smallest things – practical jokes, a plastic spider in the bed, funny stories at the meal table, hide and seek in the dark, watching a comedy film and even a water fight at 2am. Take time to laugh and have fun.

Laughter really is the best medicine.

WE ALWAYS...

None of our family are gifted photographers, but a number of years ago we were given a Sony video camera. In place of holiday snaps of children building sandcastles and playing cricket on the beach, we could capture the fun, games, fights and arguments on film in real time. We now have a large drawer full of recordings and one of our favourite pastimes, particularly on birthdays or at Christmas, is to get them out and re-live the memories. These evenings would be boring for any unsuspecting guests who might have the misfortune to be present for one of our family film nights. But to us, they are precious memories of things we used to do when the children were little. They have captured the traditions and memories that make our family unique.

Each family has its memories and traditions and they will all be different. If, as adults, we are asked to describe our childhood, more likely than not, it won't be long before we alight on a family tradition. Many families have traditions around birthdays or Christmas that are simply the way that they do things – where they hang their decorations, their favourite recipes or the order of the day's events. We have a faded birthday banner that has ceremoniously been hung in our kitchen in February, March, April, May and twice in September for the last 20 years. It is torn at the edges and stuck together with Sellotape. Last year I decided it had had its day and should be relegated to the bin. My suggestion was met with outrage from our (now grown-up) children. Apparently the banner, however faded, is an essential part of birthdays in our household. Birthdays just wouldn't be birthdays without that banner because 'we always' put it up. Suffice to say, the banner remains.

Some family traditions simply emerge of their own accord while others are created deliberately, but they all put precious deposits in our family memory bank. Our family traditions over the years have included everyone piling into our bed at 7am on birthdays, buns after school on Fridays, burger and chips on family nights, spending October half-term with the same two families, having breakfast at Tesco, singing all five verses of 'Auld Lang Syne' raucously at midnight on New Year's Eve, camping in the Quantocks, wearing silly hats to the cinema, and playing charades on Christmas Day, to name just a few. Think about what traditions you already have, and maybe even create some more. If you can't think of any, your children will help you!

Traditions and shared memories are important for children as they help build a sense of family identity, belonging – what one academic called 'a sense of connectedness' – they are unique to *us*. If we are in a blended or stepfamily then we may need to combine different ways of doing things – perhaps keeping some traditions and making new ones together – but as we do that we will find we are putting down roots and building a new identity. We are creating a 'We always … ' memory for our children's future.

LAY THE TABLE

Lay the table

In the last few years, furniture retailers have reported a drop in the sale of family dining tables.[14] Commentators surmise that the trend is due to fewer families making time to sit round a table and eat together. Busy, conflicting schedules have meant that meals on the go or in front of screens have increasingly become the norm, and smaller households are less likely to have a dining room or space for a dining table.

When our children were younger, we tried to make family meal times a priority. They were far from perfect. Children would wriggle off their chairs, poke each other, and refuse to eat what was on their plate. Water would be upset and boys would be daft with the tomato ketchup (which, according to them, can be counted as one of their 'five a day'!). Despite the mayhem, looking back, I am so glad that we persevered with having meals together as, now they are older, the routine is established and some of our best family times are around the table.

At Care for the Family we came across Jenny, a single parent mum. She said this about the importance of eating together as a family:

I have three children aged between four and ten. I work full time outside the home and life is hectic. Often the meals we eat during the week are on the run, but on Friday evenings and Sunday lunchtimes we eat 'properly' as a family.

14 djs research. *Tables are turning for dining room furniture.* http://www.marketresearchworld.net/content/view/474/77/

I've tried hard to make these meals special occasions. Each child has a task – helping with the cooking, laying the table, washing up – and although persuading the middle one to do anything at all is a battle every time, we usually get there eventually. On Fridays the meal could still be something ordinary like beans on toast, but we sit at a laid table and we talk. The telly's off.

I try not to have a go at the children during these meals – I want them to be enjoyable … Of course, getting a conversation going is sometimes like dragging teeth out – especially with the eldest one; but we've had some brilliant – and enlightening – times. Sometimes we play a game afterwards.

The other night, I got home early on a Tuesday and they'd laid the table for a 'proper' meal. One of them said, 'I know it's not the right night, Mum, but can we do it anyway?' I thought, 'Yes!'[15]

Research shows that eating together, even once a week, offers a number of benefits. It's a great opportunity for conversation – to discover what is going on in our children's lives, what they are thinking and hoping for. A simple game called 'High/Low' helped us with that. It involved taking it in turns to say what our 'high' had been for that particular day, week or month and what our 'low' had been. The children were not always co-operative, but just sometimes we heard about a falling out in the playground or an achievement on the sports field that otherwise

{ 15 p27 *The Sixty Minute Family* Rob Parsons. Lion Books (2010). }

they might not have told us about. Meal times give children the chance to grow social skills and develop language, but most importantly they encourage a sense of identity and belonging.[16]

In practical terms, having meals round the table together can be difficult to make happen. But remember that the menu doesn't need to rival *MasterChef*. Keep it simple and to budget, and give the children a sense of ownership by involving them in planning what to eat, laying the table, and the cooking itself

16 E. Cook, R. Dunifon, Parenting in Context, *Do Family Meals Really Make a Difference?* http://www.human. cornell.edu/pam/outreach/upload/Family-Mealtimes-2.pdf.

as appropriate for their age. Even a four-year-old can choose a topping and put it on a pizza.

I spoke recently to a young woman whose husband worked long hours. He was rarely home for the children's tea and meals needed to be in two or more sittings. Her tip to other parents was that, during the children's tea, instead of getting on with the jobs that were pressing – washing up, tidying the kitchen and so on – she would intentionally make a pot of tea for herself, sit down with the children and enjoy the time together.

It may not always be possible, but if we can, laying the table even once a week – with a temporary ban on mobile devices – will begin to build that sense of connection in our family life together.

THE POOREST PARENTS CAN GIVE THE BEST GIFT
– THE GIFT OF PLAY

The opening paragraph of Charlotte's first school report made for entertaining reading: 'Charlotte likes to begin the day by dressing up. Her costume of choice generally includes a pink tutu, a Viking helmet, and a feather boa.' Knowing her sense of fashion at the time, I had to smile, but I also remember thinking I would have preferred a progress report on her aptitude for reading, writing and arithmetic – the things that I considered to be the 'real' business of education.

Mrs McDonell, her teacher, no doubt had a twinkle in her eye as she penned that report. She was a wonderful teacher, colourful and expressive, a true creative with a warm, generous smile and an ample bosom, which provided refuge for many little ones in times of crisis. She loved to encourage the children to use all their senses, to imagine, to create and to play. Each of our children grew to love Mrs McD – she opened up the wonder of creation and the infinite world of the imagination, and taught them the value of an enquiring mind.

Jean Piaget, the Swiss psychologist, was particularly interested in the role of play in child development. He demonstrated that play can be an effective vehicle for children to learn about their world. He would say, 'Play is the work of children.'[17]

17 Piaget, J. (1945). *Play, dreams and imitation in childhood.* London: Heinemann.

There are a myriad of ways that children play. Building and demolishing sand castles, dressing up as pirates or princesses, pretend games of schools, shops, hospitals, mummies and daddies, games with dolls, cars, teddies, Lego, or more formal games with rules, all provide fun and enjoyment in themselves. But in addition, each aspect of play provides a relaxed atmosphere where all kinds of learning can occur and an opportunity for social skills to develop. As parents, we would do well to learn from Mrs McD not to have every minute of our child's day programmed for 'learning', but to make time for play, creativity and imagination. We might not feel that we ourselves are the creative type – or even if we were, by the time we became adults the world had knocked it out of us. We can allow our children to lead the way. They are always dreaming. Don't make them stop.

My friend Nicky's children are digital natives; they have every game, gadget and gizmo going. A 42-inch screen stretches across the living room wall, iPads, iPods and iPhones litter the floor. However, when I visited recently, they were ignoring the contents of the Apple store and were engaged in a game of make-believe. Apparently they were marooned on a desert island with Robinson Crusoe and had dragged duvets downstairs to make a raft so they could escape. They set about piling tins of beans and tuna onto the raft so they would have provisions for their time at sea.

My friend, seemingly oblivious to the resulting disarray in her kitchen cupboard, offered to swim to the shore to find the life jackets. Halfway across the ocean, she looked up and explained that this was their favourite game. And watching them play, I saw she was right. I reflected that in later life these children will remember this scene. The expensive skateboards and bikes that I passed on my way in and the electronic gadgets strewn across the floor may be fun, but nothing beats an adventure on a raft with a tin of tuna and a tin of beans and Man Friday for company.

It has been said that the poorest parents can give the best gifts – the simple gift of play and imagination.

As parents, we may attempt to buy our children expensive toys, sometimes because we didn't have them ourselves when we were young. But one expert put it well, 'We can be so busy giving our children what we didn't have that we don't have time to give them what we did have.' And that includes the simple gift of play and imagination.

The poorest parents really can give the best gifts.

"If we're going to play make believe then I'm going be the princess that sleeps for a hundred years..."

Sometimes 'playing safe' is dangerous

As a young boy growing up on the Isle of Wight, adventurer Bear Grylls was taught by his father to climb, to sail and, most importantly, to dream. His bedroom was covered in posters of Mount Everest. One day, Bear vowed to climb Everest – a dream he and his father nurtured together. His father knew the risks. Every year, the death toll on the mountain rises, and for every ten mountaineers who make it to the top, one will die. Despite the risks, however, his parents encouraged Bear's spirit of adventure, and at 7.22am on 26 May 1998, aged 23, he entered *The Guinness Book of Records* as one of the youngest climbers to reach the summit of the world's highest mountain.

Bear has since become the youngest ever Chief Scout, and around the world he is one of the most recognised faces associated with survival and outdoor adventure. His website carries the caption: 'Life is always an adventure with this man!'

While our children may not be about to join an expedition to the Himalayas, we would do well, as parents, to seek to foster in them the ability to dream and to have that same spirit of adventure.

Pick up any children's storybook, popular film or game and you are likely to discover characters involved in exciting escapades. Whether it is a gallant prince rescuing a beautiful princess from the castle, a young boy fighting a giant and winning against all the odds, a spine-tingling spy thriller or an adventure with aliens in space, we celebrate adventure. By temperament, some children will be more risk averse than others, but at heart, most delight in the thrill of adventure and new discovery. As parents, our every instinct is often to keep our children 'safe'. But if we allow that to govern our approach to parenting, always saying 'No' to any exploit that has any element of risk attached, we will be denying them the chance to develop some essential life skills.

The truth is that real adventure generally involves stepping outside the front door, away from the comfort of the living room. Find opportunities for them to have an adventure and learn new skills. It might be an organised camp or weekend away, or simply a night sleeping in a tent. It might be climbing a pole, building a fire and toasting marshmallows, constructing a den, jumping off a rock or learning to ride a bike, to skateboard or to surf a wave. Whatever it is, the exhilaration of pushing the boundaries to master new things harnesses children's natural curiosity and gives them an opportunity to be creative and develops confidence and well-being.

Wrapping them in cotton wool may mean no tumbles, plasters or trips to A & E, but unless we say 'Yes', and encourage risk-taking appropriate to their age, we will be denying our children the opportunity to build the character and resourcefulness that will enable them to dream … and then to conquer their own mountains in life.

BOUNDARIES GIVE SECURITY

Boundaries give security

It was Daniel's first day at school. He had been up since 5.30am and could hardly contain his excitement. By 8.30am the rest of the family were finally dressed and ready to go, the baby strapped into the buggy. Clutching his brand new shiny blue lunch box, Daniel hurtled out of the front door and down the path to the gate. His mum shouted at him to wait, but her entreaty fell on deaf ears. Pushing the buggy at speed, she set off down the road and tried to catch him up but to no avail – he was round the corner and out of sight in seconds. As she reached the corner she called urgently to him to wait for her at the crossing. Oblivious, he turned left and continued to sprint towards the main road where she knew that two lanes of commuter traffic would take no prisoners. Fortunately for Daniel he was not the only child walking to school that day, and his mum turned the corner in time to see him enveloped by a guardian angel wearing an ample, bright yellow high-visibility jacket, and carrying a large lollipop. After school, Daniel's mum sat him down for 'a big talk', after which he was left in no doubt about the importance of boundaries and the consequences if they were crossed.

Children need boundaries, not just for road safety but for life. And it is our job to put the boundaries in place – we are their parents, not their best friend.[18] Boundaries may be laid down to determine, for example, what films or television they can watch and when, what computer games they can play, meal times, bedtimes, standards of care for other people's belongings,

18 Kerig, Patricia. *Implications of Parent-Child Boundary Dissolution for Development Psychopathology: "Who is the Parent and Who is the Child?"* The Haworth Press, New York (2005).

expected standards of speech and behaviour. Our children's job, of course, is to push against those boundaries – that is the equation! In giving them boundaries appropriate for their age, we are giving them a gift: we will be building in them a deep sense of security that will last a lifetime.

CHOOSE YOUR STYLE

The approach parents take to setting and maintaining boundaries for their children can take different forms. At one end of the spectrum is what experts call the 'authoritarian' style. Authoritarian parents can be perfectionists at heart: they like to have lots of rules and to be in complete control. Homework has to be done before any television is allowed, meals are at set times and children are expected to sit still and finish the cauliflower on their plate. There may well be a rota on the fridge door for jobs to be done around the house and this is adhered to with military precision. Family life is fitted into fixed slots and there is little room for creativity or manœuvre. I remember one of our children stopped going to a friend's house because the parents were so strict and there were endless rules. I think he was just scared of putting a foot wrong.[19]

19 A fuller understanding of the three 'archetypal' parenting styles, as formulated by development psychologist Diana Baumrind is provided at http://www.positive-parenting-ally.com/3-parenting-styles.html

If you forget everything else, remember this.

This sheep and pen here represents the authoritarian style of parenting. The good news is that the children know clearly where the line is drawn – they know without a doubt what is and isn't allowed. However, there's a flip side to the coin. The problem with this style of parenting is that the child can feel hemmed in and controlled with no room for independent thought or to express their individuality.

Right at the other end of the spectrum is the 'permissive' approach to parenting. Children with permissive parents are often initially the envy of other children, particularly those who come from homes where authoritarian parenting is the style of choice. Their parents are chilled and relaxed, there are few boundaries and if they are crossed there are no consequences. The children decide whether or not to do their homework and there are no limits on screen time. Meal times are whenever people are hungry and there's no requirement for the children to sit still, to eat cauliflower or in fact to do anything they don't want to do that day. Jobs are done by whoever is around at the time, and family life is chaotic but carefree. The mantra of these parents is: 'Do what you like.'

This second sheep illustrates the permissive style of parenting. The good news is that the child has complete freedom to explore and discover things for themselves. However, the disadvantage of parenting in this way is that the child can feel lost and lonely. Our children need boundaries, if only to push against. Boundaries give security.

Finally, in the middle of the parenting style spectrum – and something to aim for – is the 'assertive' style. Assertive parents know the importance of setting boundaries, but set as few rules as possible. The rules that they do set are enforced. For example, they lay down guidelines about homework (generally it is to be done before watching television), but they are prepared to agree exceptions when a reasonable request is made. They monitor their children's screen time and negotiate it with them. There is a routine for family meals – children are expected to sit at the table and to try to eat everything, but the parents will compromise over some things (usually cauliflower). As a general rule, family members are expected to help clear the table, but this can be relaxed as agreed – for example, when the child's friend comes round. They give their children a clear understanding of what they expect, give explanations and listen to opposing views. This style of parenting is sometimes described as 'firm but fair'.

The third picture illustrates the assertive style of parenting. Children can see where the boundaries are and so feel safe, accepted and loved. They have room to explore, to grow in independence and to push against the boundaries in the knowledge that they are there for their benefit.

Our approach to parenting will be influenced by the way we have been parented ourselves, as well as by our individual temperament and personality. With the benefit of hindsight, most of us will look back and regret having either laid down the law too firmly or been too relaxed on a specific issue. None of us will get this right all of the time. The pithy statement, 'Rules without relationship lead to rebellion' is well put. If we can simply aim for the assertive parenting style – to be firm and fair in the context of a good relationship with our children – we will be giving them a secure base from which to explore the world.

And just a word on these issues to those parenting children with additional needs. Whether an apparently 'mild' condition or more complex, parents of children with additional needs face a whole set of unique challenges and experiences which can place extra demands on the family. These children have the same need for boundaries. They will feel loved, safe and secure when they know what is expected of them. As a parent try to have realistic expectations of your child's behaviour – not too high (but not too low either!). Maggie Stapleton manages Care for the Family's Additional Needs Support project. Reflecting on the challenges faced by parents in this area she commented:

> *A family with an additional needs child is like any other family … but with 'extras'. As tempting as it is, when setting boundaries try not to be overprotective. If we wrap our children in cotton wool the danger is that they won't learn new skills and we make them more dependent on us than they need to be.*

Knowing what our natural parenting style is will help us understand some of the struggles we may be having. The main difficulty in setting boundaries with children with additional needs is communication – you may can feel you are having to say the same thing time and again; bucketloads of patience and understanding is required and sometimes the ability to reassess what is really important and to let some things go.

CHOOSE YOUR BATTLES

Choose your battles

As someone who can veer towards the authoritarian style of parenting, one of the most helpful pieces of wisdom I received was, 'Choose your battles.'

There are so many potential battles we could have: 'Tidy your bedroom', 'Eat your crusts', 'Keep the water in the bath', 'Wear your coat to school', 'Put your toys away', 'Come to the table', 'Keep out of the puddles', 'Brush your hair', 'Clean your teeth', 'Learn your spellings', 'Hang up your bag', 'Don't pinch your sister'. Because the list is endless, if we make every issue a battle to fight not only will we wear ourselves out, but more importantly, our children will never learn which things are *really* important.

As a family, we spent a memorable October half-term staying with friends in their beautiful harbour-side cottage in Cornwall. We planned to mark the final evening by going out for a meal. The restaurant we chose was across the estuary, and so instead of driving round by car we decided to add to the fun of the evening by piling into their small dingy and sailing across to the other side. We agreed to meet on the jetty at 6.30pm.

The autumn air meant that by 6.30 it was quite chilly. We had dressed up for the occasion and, undeterred, put on an extra layer and went down to the jetty.

Everyone, that is, except our third son, Ed, who was then six. He had a new, full-length wetsuit, and his six-year-old logic was that, if we were going in a boat, a wetsuit was the correct thing to wear. In contrast, my adult reasoning told me that everyone else had dressed up for dinner and wetsuits were for the beach. Despite my best efforts, Ed refused to be persuaded to change. At 6.45, with the rest of the party getting colder by the minute waiting for our arrival, I paused and asked myself the question: is this a battle I need to fight? And so down we went to the jetty and over to the restaurant, Ed in a wetsuit and everyone else dressed for an evening out.

It was a hilarious evening that we still remember. Ed did overheat, and getting in and out of the wetsuit when he visited the loo caused a queue that rivalled Harrods' sale. But looking back, we nearly missed out on the fun of the evening, and the memory we'd carry with us for years to come, by my choosing to have a battle that wasn't really worth fighting.

Correct clothing for a meal out may be a battle you want to fight. If it is, stay firm and fight it tooth and nail. But be careful, because you will almost certainly have far more important battles to fight further down the road. Decide what things are important to you, then say 'Yes' to as many of your children's requests as possible, and 'No' to the rest.

Choose your battles.

"I've refined our chosen battle strategy and will be ready to de-brief at 0-eight hundred. Roger that?"

SAY WHAT YOU MEAN AND MEAN WHAT YOU SAY

Say what you mean and mean what you say

If we set a clear boundary in place and our children either sneak across it quietly or march defiantly over it, it is vital that there are consequences. If we simply turn a blind eye our children will soon come to believe that we don't say what we mean or mean what we say.

I remember learning that lesson from another mum. Our eldest child, George, had been to play at a friend's house and in their living room were two enormous beanbags, full of polystyrene balls. A recent visit to see Father Christmas had evidently kicked the two boys' creative genes into overdrive and inspired them to invent a wonderful game. They had opened the beanbag, tipped out all the polystyrene balls and made what they called a 'Winter Wonderland'.

Under the misguided belief that they were happily occupied playing Lego, my friend had enjoyed a moment of peace and quiet, and when she put her head round the door later was ill-prepared for the re-landscaping of her living room that had occurred. Kirsty Allsop would have been proud. Several hours later the Hoover had made little inroad into the scene of devastation, as the polystyrene balls gained a static electricity of their own. She was definitely not impressed! She let the boys know in no uncertain terms that this game was never to happen again and, in fact, if it was repeated, George would be sent straight home.

A fortnight later, when they were playing together at the same house, the boys decided to take a chance. They opened the beanbags again and a second snow scene was created that was even more splendid than the first. But this mum had set a boundary and had spelled out the consequence of crossing it. Before the boys could blink, she terminated the game and returned a shocked and sheepish-looking George to our doorstep. That day those boys learnt that when that mummy said something, she meant it. Although there were many more moments of creative play that often involved duvets, towels, chairs and the contents of the food cupboard, they never did open up the beanbags again.

We were at a neighbour's lunchtime birthday party just after Christmas. A young mum, Anna, had been invited along with her three children, a six-year-old girl and twin four-year-old boys. The number of people meant that the party overflowed into the garden, and we gathered around an open fire, which provided welcome warmth in the sub-zero temperatures. As we chatted, Anna's twins came running towards the fire. She caught them by the hand, bent down to their level, looked them in the eye and put on a very solemn voice. She showed them a line on the paving stone on the ground and explained to them they could go up to that line, but not an inch further. If anyone went over the line, they would have to leave the party. Two little red heads nodded in agreement. One twin stayed firmly where he was, but the other looked her straight the eye and deliberately put the toe of his trainer a centimetre over the mark. That little boy was saying to his mother, 'I wonder how much you really mean what you say?' And fortunately for him, he discovered she did. For that four-year-old, the party ended early that day.

One mum contacted us at Care for the Family and told us about a time when her daughter had been misbehaving, and she turned to her and said, 'If you do that one more time then we won't be going to *The Lion King*. Her daughter did it again.

That mum then had a problem. They had already bought tickets for *The Lion King*, they were going with another family, and they were booked on a coach to London. As they arrived at the theatre and her daughter made her way down the aisle with a large bag of sweets in one hand and a bucket of popcorn in the other, she realised that it had not been the most effective consequence she could have come up with!

Say what you mean and mean what you say – and just make sure you can really follow through on the consequences!

"ONE. TWO.
TWO AND A HALF.
TWO AND THREE QUARTERS,..
... TWO AND NINETEEN
          TWENTIETHS,
             TWO AND... "

REMEMBER THE THREE Ds

Remember the three Ds

Sitting round a campfire on a weekend away, we struck up a conversation with a family friend who was now a grandfather. He and his family had been through some challenging times and, as the night drew in, he shared with us some of the lessons learnt along the way. In talking about boundaries and discipline, he told us about a framework that had been helpful to them. He called it 'the principle of the three Ds' and soon after that we adopted it into our family life.

He explained to us that there were three behaviours all beginning with the letter 'D' that were out of bounds for their family. They were:

Dishonesty   *Disrespect*   *Disobedience*

He described the three Ds as being like three sides of a triangle. His children were free to do anything they liked within the triangle but must not cross those three thresholds. The three things were based on the things they believed were important to them as a family:

Honesty – *so there would be consequences for telling lies or other dishonesty. For example, claiming to have cleaned your teeth when the toothbrush was still dry, or for secretly* *eating a chocolate from your brother's Advent calendar. A failure to own up would always be treated more seriously than the original misdemeanour.*

Respect – *for other people and their possessions – so there were consequences for rudeness, thoughtlessness and disrespect. For example, refusing to thank Mrs Jones for tea, or for giving your sister's doll a tattoo with a permanent pen.*

Obedience – *so there were consequences for deliberately being disobedient. For example, throwing a cricket ball in the kitchen (in the knowledge that the deal was it was for garden use only) or refusing to turn off the tv and come to the table for a meal when asked.*

Different families will have different things they believe are important, so decide what things are important to you. Once you have done this, find a way of communicating them to your children so that they know where they stand. We found over the years that although the three Ds was a simple formula, it covered almost every eventuality, and when it came to setting boundaries, it wasn't a bad place to start.

"OK. I've created a simple set of principles we're all going to live by. I call it the 4 As, the 6 Bs, 7 Cs 2 Ds, 8 Es ..."
?

CHILDISH IRRESPONSIBILITY

OR

DISOBEDIENCE

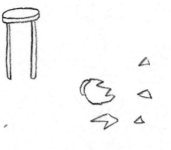

Childish irresponsibility or disobedience?

If your child has crossed a boundary, before reacting it can be helpful to press the pause button and ask yourself, 'Are they simply acting their age?' In other words, are they old enough to have understood the boundary and the consequence, or does their action simply reflect their immaturity? Is this a childish act for which they are not responsible or are they actually being disobedient?

Our family had been invited to a wedding, and to avoid an early start we arranged to stay with friends the night before. Breakfast the next morning was accompanied with shouts of joy and delight from our boys as their eyes alighted on a giant box of Coco Pops. Chocolate cereal in our house was a very special treat reserved for high days and holidays, and they couldn't believe their good fortune! In the excitement, little hands weren't big enough to grasp the packet, and in less than a nanosecond chocolate cereal and milk spilt everywhere, including all down the wedding shirts that, in a misguided moment of hope over experience, I had suggested they wore for breakfast.

Frustrating and annoying as it was, I only had myself to blame. They were excited and the disaster was the result of childish high spirits rather than disobedience or naughtiness – they couldn't be expected to know that they couldn't hold the packet.

A few months later Coco Pops featured again. On the Monday morning I made a trip to Sainsbury's to buy a packet for a special birthday breakfast the following Wednesday. The whole family knew that the Coco Pops were for the birthday breakfast and not for general consumption. So on Tuesday morning when I discovered that not only had the cereal been opened and eaten, but (adding insult to injury) the free toy dinosaur inside had been taken from the packet, my reaction was very different to the one I had on the day of wedding. One of our children had been deliberately disobedient. They knew what they were doing and they knew there would be consequences.

In the heat of the moment it can be easy to overreact, but just pausing for a moment to consider whether our children are being deliberately naughty or simply acting their age can mean that we respond appropriately to their actions.

LABEL THE ACTION, NEVER THE CHILD

The children's playground rhyme, 'Sticks and stones may break my bones but words will never hurt me' is simply not true. Most of us can remember only too well hurtful words that have been spoken to us. When our children are testing us to the limit it can be so easy to slip into saying things that not only convey our frustration or anger at what they have done, but also label their character.

I came across the following letter, which underlines the importance of the way we speak to our children.

My father left our family home when I was young and we lost touch with him. I will never know if he ever tried to get in touch, but if he did, my mother kept it from us. When I was just ten, my mother died suddenly and unexpectedly. I was sent to live with my great-aunt. I can understand it, as the last thing she needed was a ten-year-old to look after, but she never made me feel welcome. She told me repeatedly that I was a nuisance and in the way. Looking back, the impact of her words has shaped who I am. As an adult I have low self-esteem and little confidence. I am working to change that, but I believe my life could have been so different if, in those early years, those who cared for me had pointed out what was right with me rather than what was wrong.

My daughter recalls a time at junior school when she was given the chance to try a number of new activities – Brownies, swimming, ballet, recorder and drama club, to name just a few. She embraced these opportunities wholeheartedly – only to want to give each up after the first term. As a parent, I thought I detected a pattern of behaviour in her that would make life difficult for her later. Spotting a 'learning opportunity' I said to her, 'Don't be a quitter, persevere. Don't give up!' But what I had thought was a call to arms and an exhortation to aim high, she saw as a rebuke. It was years later that she told me that the words that she heard me say were, 'You are a quitter.' The power of those words shaped how she saw herself, and it took her several years to believe otherwise.

I know that in the heat of the moment I have sometimes used words carelessly to my children. Rather than commenting on them – 'You are so selfish/unkind/naughty … (fill in the blank)' – we would do well to describe their *behaviour*. So instead of, 'You were so unkind to leave Lottie out of your game' we might say, 'When you wouldn't let Lottie join in your game, that was an unkind thing to do.' In describing their behaviour it leaves open the possibility of change.

We all wear labels from our past; some are easier to read than others. As parents we have an important role in shaping our children's character and bringing correction when it is needed. But as we do that, let's ensure that above all, what they hear loudly and clearly are positive words that will form their identity and build their character for years to come.

CONSEQUENCES ARE THE BEST TEACHERS

As I write this chapter, my phone beeps to announce the arrival of a text message. It is from son number three who has gone to play football with friends. The text (very politely) asks whether, if I am not doing anything, I can 'pop over' with his forgotten football boots? My reply on this occasion? 'Sorry, no'.

By the time our children near the end of junior school, most parents will undoubtedly have had similar requests. As well as numerous appeals for forgotten items of sports equipment, I have had requests for cookery ingredients, recorder music, bus fares, inhalers, homework, packed lunches and a host of things besides. Depending on the circumstances, the age of the child, and their history in this area, as well the consequences of not having the item in question (the inhaler was delivered pronto!), sometimes the answer has been 'Yes' and sometimes 'No'. As parents, our natural instinct is to make life as easy as possible for our children – we don't like seeing them make and suffer the consequences of mistakes – but sometimes in life, lessons are best learnt the hard way.

'The helicopter parent'[20] is a term used to describe the overprotective parent – the mum or dad who hovers overhead,

20 E. Lee, J. Bristow, C. Faircloth and J. Macvarish, Parenting Culture Studies. Palgrave Macmillan, Hampshire (2014).

paying close attention to their child's every need and swoops in at every turn to prevent catastrophe. Forgotten sports kit or other items are delivered immediately, excuses are provided for a failure to do music practice, and homework is done by proxy. Helicopter parents operate from the very best of intentions, wanting to protect their offspring from the knocks of life, but the results often put their children at a disadvantage.

Resilience is the ability to handle the everyday frustrations, challenges and disappointments that life throws at us and to bounce back from them. Our children are born with the capacity for resilience, and as parents we are the most important people to help build and develop this quality in their lives.

Having the resolve to sometimes let our children learn the hard way has the power to unleash resourcefulness, resilience

"That's Jane Simmons. She's taking Helicopter parenting to the next level..."

and creativity in them – qualities which will stand them in good stead in years to come. Out of the many times son number three has forgotten his kit, he has yet to miss the match. Where there is a will there is usually a way!

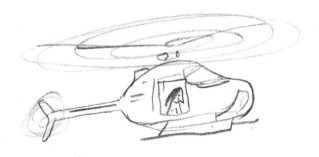

SHOULDER
TO
SHOULDER

Shoulder to shoulder

Back in the 1970s there was a TV series called *Shoulder to Shoulder*. It told the story of Emmeline Pankhurst and her fellow suffragettes as they campaigned at the turn of the 20th century for the right for women to vote. One of the reasons they were able to make an impact was their singular unity of purpose.

'Shoulder to shoulder' is not a bad mantra for couples parenting together. We need to have that same determination to stand united in all matters of discipline. If one parent is seen as a 'soft touch', or if there is a chink of light between you, most single-minded youngsters will be able to use it to their advantage. Even if we disagree with a line taken by the other parent, a show of unity is vital.

Joy asked six-year-old Daniel to clear up his Lego before tea. Tea-time came and went and the Lego remained strewn across the floor. An hour later Daniel found himself being sent to bed without any pudding. When dad, Sam, came home he went upstairs to say goodnight and heard the sorry tale. Daniel omitted to tell him he had polished off a plate of spaghetti and spun the yarn that, having been unjustly denied his yoghurt, he was still hungry. Sam swallowed the entire story and within minutes was delivering a couple of digestives to his son, undermining Joy and her attempt to exercise assertive parenting by following through on consequences.

There have been occasions when, in the heat of the moment, either Richard or I have meted out a draconian punishment that does not fit the crime. At those times it has been a challenge for the other one of us not to commiserate with our child at the unfairness of the situation, rather than simply discussing it afterwards with each other.

If we are parenting with our child's mother or father, but living apart, it is an extra challenge, but seeking to be of one mind is vital. And if we are bringing up our children alone it can feel exhausting to be the one who continually has to set and maintain boundaries. In this situation it is important to find friends who can help and support you – a community that can encourage you in this most important of roles.

ENJOY THE GENERATION GAME

Wednesday afternoons were a special day for our elder two children. When they were at primary school we were fortunate to have their grandparents living nearby, and Wednesday was the day the children would visit them for tea. Their grandfather would meet them at the school gate and then walk them home via the bakery, where they would spend hours choosing two small cakes. After rehearsing all the options at length (my father is a very patient man!), they would almost always make the same choices: a pink cake with a strawberry on the top for Charlotte and anything large with chocolate and quantities of cream for George. The cakes would be ceremoniously placed into a box and taken to their grandparents' house where they would be readily consumed.

The children would spend the next hour reading stories, doing jigsaw puzzles and playing cards and traditional board games such as Snakes and Ladders and Checkers, games that never seemed to lose their appeal. They look back on those afternoons with great fondness, not least because of the foundation that was laid for their relationship with their grandparents.

Their other grandparents lived further away, but also played a vital part in our children's upbringing. They invested in them in so many ways, but particularly when they were older. They would have one child at a time for 'special' visits, including what became a much-anticipated trip to Cadbury World.

I wonder what images are conjured up in your mind as you consider the word 'Grandparent'. It could be a round, bespectacled old lady wiping the flour from her hands as she puts the finishing touches to the Victoria sponge, a lady in a bed with rather large teeth talking to a small girl in red, or perhaps somebody more fearsome altogether. But whatever view we may have, the truth is that modern grandparents are varied in the extreme. There are grandmothers who are natives to Facebook and tweet daily, there are sky-diving granddads, career ladder-climbing Nannie, Bampas, Poppas or whatever other tags get attached to the older members of our families. (Incidentally, a little tip, just in case you ever become a grandparent: be careful what you allow them to call you in the first few weeks after they first 'name' you – because you will be stuck with it for life.)

But as well as a great variety of grandparents in life-style, there are differences emotionally. Some people cannot wait until they become grandparents – and adopt the title and the role as though they are born to it. Others are not at all sure they are ready (or old enough!) for this task and actually a little nervous as to whether they will measure up.

But at their best, there is no doubt that grandparents can have wonderful influence on the lives of their grandchildren, and as parents, even if family relationships are complicated, it is worth making the effort to give the opportunity to enable that to happen. One eight-year-old put it like this, 'Everybody should have a grandmother – because they're the only grown-ups that have time.' One academic called the relationship between grandparents and grandchildren 'an unemotionally uncomplicated form of love.' If that is true then it has to do with the fact that generally they do not bear ultimate responsibility for the child: in other words they can enjoy their grandchildren's good traits without feeling guilty about the bad ones. And perhaps it is that very lack of ultimate responsibility that can allow grandparents to truly give the gift of unconditional love – they are not trying to get all that homework in on time, the recorder practice done, or having to demand that the hamster is at least found – if not fed. One child said, 'Being with my gran is like having a bath that is full of bubbles and with no cold bits.'

But perhaps, above all, grandparents can help a child answer some of the deepest questions: 'Who am I?' 'Do I belong?' and 'What is my place in the world?' So much of that has to do with discovering *roots* – and grandparents are wonderful for that. There's an old African saying, 'When an old person dies it's as if a library burns down.' But the library shouldn't burn down. I didn't know my grandparents, and watching my children now and their relationship with their grandparents I see now just what I missed out on growing up. If your parents are alive, encourage them to tell the stories of when they were children, share old photographs and if possible take your children to places that were important to them – their school, their home, their workplace. Lois Wyse said, 'Grandparents connect the dots from generation to generation.'

But before we get too starry-eyed, let's be honest enough to admit that there can be problems with grandparents – and generally in two areas: too near and too far away. We all know stories of rogue grandparents who interfere, criticise or, as in one spectacular piece of misjudgement we came across, announce – 'Great news I've just agreed to buy the other half of your semi! I wanted to surprise you.' I think it's fair to say that she achieved that, although her son and daughter-in-law had the last laugh when three months later they agreed to buy the other half of somebody else's!

'Too near' needn't just be a geographical thing – more that grandparents can be simply interfering. And perhaps here above all we need the wisdom of Solomon. On the one hand perhaps we can afford to be understanding and realise that they have all this hard won experience of raising children but, frustratingly for them, just about the time they got the hang of it – they were redundant. But wise grandparents know that in truth their role has changed: they have moved from being the coach at the side of the track to shouting encouragement from the grandstand. And whilst listening to advice graciously given, we have to have confidence in our own parenting – our children are *our* responsibility.

Then there's the problem of 'too far away' – although it's harder, grandparenting at a distance needn't be as daunting as it may seem at first – but it does need a bit more ingenuity!

We know grandparents who, in their eighties, have mastered the wonders of email, texting and Skype for the sake of staying in touch with their grandchildren. One granddad, who lives thousands of miles from his children, said, 'Of course I would love them to be closer but because we try harder I'm sure we "see" more of them than many grandparents who live around the corner.' A family who grandparent not just across miles but across time zones, set up an iPad and Facetime their grandchildren during Sunday lunch, which coincides with the grandchildren's breakfast. Another grandfather bought two copies of a fairy story and sent one to his grandchild. Once a week, the grandfather reads the story down the phone to the six-year-old child who follows the pictures in his book. Another grandmother has created a storybook with her grandson. She has written one chapter and then sent it to him to complete the next. Yet another grandparent reminded me that even – and perhaps especially – in this technological age children love to receive letters – a real piece of paper, with real writing and your very own name on the envelope is enough to make any eight-year-old feel special.

There are numerous ways of staying in touch but my favourite is a little idea devised by a grandmother for her small granddaughter and quoted in Rob Parsons' book 'The Sixty Minute Grandparent.' [21] She made a brightly coloured wrap that had an outline of her own hands at either end. She told her granddaughter that at any time she could ask her mum to curl it around her and she would feel her Granny's arms hugging her. She had no idea how important the present would become to a very insistent two-year-old. Every night, just as her grandmother who lives in Scotland is waking up, a small child in Sydney, Australia falls off to sleep with her grandmother's 'arms' wrapped tightly around her.

It is true that grandparents can be a wonderful influence on our children but it's not all one way. Ruth Goode put it beautifully: 'Our grandchildren accept us for ourselves, without

21 Rob Parsons. *The Sixty Minute Grandparent*. Hodder & Stoughton (2013). http://www.careforthefamily.org.uk/shop/parenting-books/sixty-minute-grandparent

rebuke or effort to change us, as no one in our entire lives has ever done, not our parents, siblings, spouses, friends – and hardly ever our own grown children'.

But it was Sam Levenson who managed to identify the reason for the magic that is so often found in this relationship: 'The reason Grandparents and Grandkids get along so well is because they have a common enemy.'

I think there's some truth in that!

BE THE
FIRST
TO SAY
SORRY

Be the first to say sorry

An Oscar for the worst catchphrase ever must surely go to the 1970s novel and film *Love Story* with 'Love means never having to say you're sorry.' In fact, for all relationships, including that of parent and child, the reverse is true. Loving our children means *often* having to say we are sorry. Being able to recognise when we are in the wrong and to apologise for it is one of the most important lessons that we can hand on to our children.

When my children were small, I can remember many occasions when I sent them to the 'naughty step' and told them to consider the error of their ways. After a suitable time of self-examination and reflection – one minute for each year of their age – they would need to apologise to their sibling, to their father, to me, or whoever it was they had wronged. But I also remember times when Richard or I overstepped the line in getting cross with them.

On one occasion, while one of our children was doing time on the step, I remember thinking that my reaction had been far from perfect, and I would do well to sit on the naughty step myself and consider *my* behaviour! At bedtime that night, I said sorry to the child in question and asked for their forgiveness. In later years they have told me how powerful that lesson was for them.

Whether we are the child or the parent we will make mistakes, and, intentionally or not, we will hurt others. The old proverb says 'love prospers when a fault is forgiven'. If we, as their parents, demonstrate that we try to seek forgiveness quickly and don't keep a record of wrongs, we will enable our children to build healthy relationships themselves in years to come. So lead the way – be the first to say 'Sorry'.

TAKE A WALK IN HIS MOCCASINS

We would do well to take one of our parenting proverbs from the Native Americans. In passing on wisdom to the next generation they would encourage their children not to judge anyone 'until you have walked two moons in his moccasins'. Our cultural equivalent might be 'to stand in someone else's shoes'. It neatly describes the quality of empathy – the ability to see a situation through someone else's eyes, to be understanding of their feelings and their needs. As parents it is good to try to encourage empathy in our children.[22]

I discovered quickly that it can be hard work trying to teach our children to share and to think of others. Any thoughts of sitting back and enjoying a catch-up and coffee with another mum while the boys played happily together, sharing the contents of the box of cars, bricks or tub of Lego, generally remained a dream. There was a season of life when two of our children seemed to spend most of their time arguing about anything and everything. If my back was turned for a second there would be a blood curdling scream of 'It's not *faaaair!* He – or she – hit me/bit me/kicked me.' I frequently wondered where

22 Weissbourd, R. and Jones, S. *How Parents Can Cultivate Empathy in Children.* Harvard Graduate School of Education. http://sites.gse.harvard.edu/sites/default/files/making-caring-common/files/empathy.pdf.

we had gone wrong to have children who seemed unable to play nicely together. My skills as a referee became honed to rival those of the refs in the Premier League: yellow card warnings and the occasional red card send-off were used to try to resolve disputes and to keep the peace.

If you are at a stage in parenting when an uninterrupted coffee is nothing more than a distant dream, stick with it. This important quality of empathy comes from the relationship we, or their primary carer, have with our children during these formative years when we are trying to encourage them to see things from another's perspective.

I have a friend who has five children and has somehow engendered this generous spirit into her children from a young age. She tells me there is no magic formula – but that she has simply consistently and continually tried to model this attitude in her own life, and then also encouraged her children to do the same. She has asked them questions like: 'How do you think Katy feels not getting the part in the play?' or, 'Do you think what's going on for Jack at home means he's not very happy? Maybe that's why he was unkind today?' or, slightly further afield, 'Can you imagine how cold it must be for Ian selling the Big Issue in the snow?' Whilst she may of course be blessed with compliant children, there is no doubt that her attitude has paid off. Like any family they have their moments, but overall they are some of the most kind and thoughtful children that I know.

As our children get older we can spot opportunities to help them develop this quality. We can talk to them about difficult friendships in the playground, about issues of sibling rivalry, or ask them to consider the situations of those less fortunate than themselves, helping them to see things from another's point of view.

As parents, the task of reinforcing good behaviour can sometimes feel relentless, so in those rare moments when we get a glimpse of the fruit of our efforts, it is even more rewarding. I have shared a number of our family's mistakes; allow me now to share an encouragement. It was a freezing day in January when we went to visit family in Birmingham. On the way home we stopped for a pizza. The waitress came and took our order, but there was a mix up, and to his delight, one of our children ended up with not one but two giant pizzas. Not even he could eat both, and so we arranged to take it away in a box, planning to eat it in the car on the way home.

We put on coats and had just left the restaurant when my son stopped in his tracks and ran across the road. I saw him give the pizza to a homeless person who was sheltering from the cold in a doorway. And as he gave it to the man, I saw him smile, look the man in the eye and touch him on the arm. It was such a kind and generous gesture – and, at that particular moment in our parenting journey, such an encouragement for us to see that quality of empathy emerging in this child's life. At that moment I was proud of him ... and I think heaven smiled as well.

SLOW DOWN

YOU'RE MOVING

Slow down, you're moving too fast!

Many of us as parents can look back to 'light bulb' moments, times when we see life in a different way, and which cause us to draw a line in the sand and resolve to live differently thereafter. Such a moment occurred for us when our children were five, seven, nine and eleven. Keen for them to be proficient in the water, I had made enquiries about swimming lessons. Other mums at school had recommended an excellent teacher called Kim who ran classes on a Monday after school. The only drawback was that it was at a school pool on the far side of the city. Even more inconvenient was the fact that, because of their range of age and ability, the lessons for our four children would have to be separate – one after the other. This meant that every Monday we had to dash straight from school through rush-hour traffic, in order to set up camp in the hot, steamy, chlorine-filled atmosphere of the pool for several hours.

I would pass the time by taking a packed tea and getting the younger children to do their reading while the older children swam, but it did not make for the most restful start to the week. However, I was determined they should learn to swim and this seemed to be the only way to make it happen. Head down and blinkered, I persevered.

Before long the children were asking to do other after-school activities that 'everyone else' was doing: Brownies, Beavers, Cubs, judo, recorder, football, tennis, netball, drama and – the straw that broke the camel's back – gymnastics. Each of the activities required a trip in the car to deliver and collect the child/children and extra friends, and soon every day of the week was taken up with some activity. Not all of these cost money, but all cost time. Without us making a conscious decision, we had drifted into living at an unsustainable pace. The activities were fun, but there was no time just to 'be'.

The light bulb moment came when I listened to someone

"ok daddy, I can fit you in for a cuddle on Thursday at 3.20. Does that work for you?"

giving a talk entitled 'Rhythms of life'. The speaker talked about the tyranny of busyness and the frantic pace of life that we lead, which not only takes its toll on us, but sucks everyone around us into our spinning vortex.

As he spoke, my mind reflected on the Monday swimming marathon and other after-school activities that came a close second, and I resolved to make some changes to our family life. We are fortunate to live near the centre of our community, so taking that into account, my decision was to limit activities to those we could walk to. Any activity that involved strapping four children in the car and driving across the city, pressing through rush-hour traffic and then going through the entire procedure in reverse, would stop.

This simple decision changed our lives. We found a swimming teacher at the local school, and although she may not have been as experienced or qualified as the excellent Kim, she did the job we wanted. While our children will never be in the Olympic swimming squad, they do all have badges on their towels as proof that they learnt to stay afloat, and we achieved it without imploding in the process.

Different families will have different pressures on their time and energies. There may be some things that are important and that we definitely want our children to do, and others that we are not so concerned about. The important thing is to find a rhythm that works for you in your particular season of family life. If you live apart from your child's other parent and the child's time is divided between two homes, it will be even more important to monitor their pace. Those parenting alone will generally be the sole decision-maker and provider of the resources to make any activities happen, and they may need to be even more ruthless in choosing what they can and cannot do. They may also need to be prepared to ask for help and support where necessary.

An unsustainable pace of life can creep up on us unawares. Take a stock check and ask yourself if you can keep going with your rhythm of life. If necessary, take drastic action to change things. Your children may not be at every club and activity, but you and they will have time to *be*.

IT
TAKES
A
VILLAGE

It takes a village

I don't believe there ever was a 'golden age' of the family, but I do believe that bringing up children was easier when families lived near each other and they could rely on the wisdom and support of the extended family. In our society, over the last fifty years, family life has changed immensely. Geographical distance, family breakdown, multiple caring responsibilities, and the long-hours culture have all contributed to there being less connectedness between extended families. Isolation and loneliness are increasingly the hallmarks of our society – not just for the elderly, but for many younger people as well. Half a century ago, if a young mum had a baby who wouldn't sleep, if a newly-married couple had the row of a century, or a child needed advice with a school project, there would most likely have been a grandparent, an uncle, an aunt or a cousin just down the road who would be able to give much-needed reassurance, advice and support. But today many are parenting without family or even friends nearby, and we are the poorer for it.

I know that in some ways we have more communication possibilities at our disposal than ever, but I also know through my work that many parents feel incredibly isolated in their role of bringing up children. One mum put it like this, 'I've got good friends and neighbours but I don't feel I can ask them about problems I am facing with the kids: I'd either feel that if I was a "proper" mother I would know the answer or feel disloyal for sharing the difficulty outside the home. It's never earth shattering stuff – and it's not that there's not loads of material in magazines or on the web – it's just having someone talk to – somebody to say, "This is not just you – you're doing a great job."'

There is a lovely African proverb: 'It takes a village to raise a child.' African culture recognises that parenting is a shared responsibility – a communal affair – not just the concern of parents or grandparents, but of the extended family. Uncles, aunts, cousins, neighbours and friends can all be involved and all have a part to play.

As 21st-century families, we have much to learn from the people of Africa. Even if we do not have extended family of our own on our doorstep, we can be 'family' to others in our community, giving and receiving mutual help and support. Especially when the children are small, get all the help you can!

When each of our children were small, I sought out friends

with children of a similar age, and arranged to spend time together. An unintended consequence was that our children benefitted from being part of another family and seeing how things were done differently. When the children were little, a local parent and toddler group was a life-line – especially when a few of us decided we'd had enough of the 'Mine's already walking/talking/doing calculus' routine. We started being honest with each other: what a relief to discover that tantrums, whining and foot stamping were normal – and that was just the mothers! We also made friends with those who had children just a little older than ours. They were able to give us the benefit of their experience through some of the ordinary, and also extraordinary, moments of family life – remedies for unexplained rashes and allergies; tips for dealing with a child who wouldn't eat anything green, or one who accidentally swallowed a button; and advice about which school to apply for and how to appeal when you don't get your first choice … and so on.

'It takes a village to raise a child.' Different people have joined our 'village' throughout our journey as parents, and no doubt there will be more to come – extended family, friends, godparents, single people, married people, pensioners and students. Our lives – and the lives of our children – and we hope their lives too – have been the richer for it.[23]

The truth of all this is beautifully expressed by another saying from Africa – this time from the Sukuma tribe from Tanzania: 'One knee does not bring up a child.'

Find those other knees!

23 Jo Griffen, (2010). Mental Health Foundation: *The Lonely Society?* http://www.mentalhealth.org.uk/content/assets/pdf/publications/the_lonely_society_report.pdf.

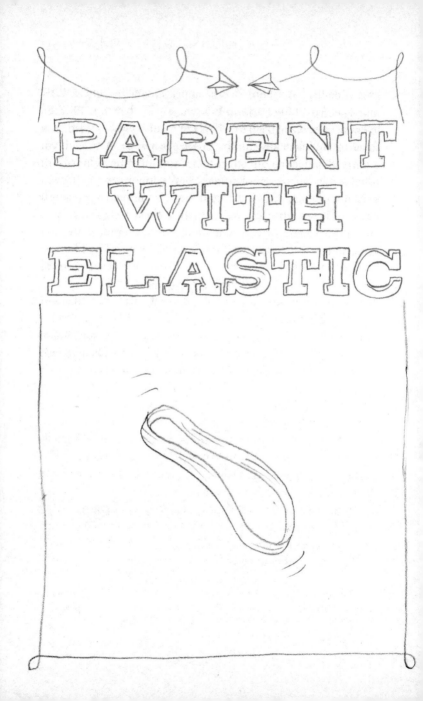

Parent with elastic

Looking back, many of us will remember specific moments when our children took a significant step to independence. The feelings we had the first time we left them with a babysitter, the first sleepover, the first day at school or the first trip to town may be etched on our minds. We know that our task as parents is to encourage our children to move from dependence to independence, but it can be so hard!

As parents we're hardwired to protect our children. It's as if we want to keep them on the end of a tight piece of string to make sure they stay safe and are equipped for every eventuality. But a wise friend once said to me, 'Don't use string, use elastic.' If we use string from the beginning, then as they seek their independence, that string will go taut and eventually snap. But if we use elastic, it will gradually stretch as we give them more responsibility as they grow up.

I like the idea of parenting with elastic. It makes the road to independence much easier for our children and also for us. From the day they take those first few faltering steps, we are beginning a process that will ultimately end with them standing on their own two feet long-term.

We can start this process when they are quite young by offering a choice of two alternatives for everyday occurrences. For example, 'Do you want your drink in the blue cup or the yellow cup?' 'Would you like peas or beans for tea?' 'Do you want to take your bike or your scooter to the park?' We can then move on to giving them limited choices, such as what to wear

– even if the pink flowery, orange check, red spots and green striped combination will require sunglasses all round.

As they get older we can give them freedom to choose how to spend pocket money, what colour to paint their room, what music they listen to, how to spend their time.

In giving our children limited choices appropriate to their age, we also give them the freedom to learn from the consequences of their decisions, which nudges them further along the road to independence. A friend who is a childminder teaches this to the children in her care: 'You can choose to put your wellies on now – good choice – and we can go out to the park. Or you can continue to lie on the floor – bad choice – and we will run out of time and not be able to go.' The key here is that if we give our children the choice, we need to be OK with either option – not always easy! I remember allowing my daughter to choose what to wear for a big family celebration when all the great aunts, uncles and grannies would be there. I had to bite my lip hard as she came down the stairs all dressed up and ready to go in a flowery summer dress, a stripy cardigan, spotty socks and her very favourite shoes – big, black patent Dr Marten boots with rainbow laces!

In my mind's eye I had imagined her wearing her flowery dress, but with a plain navy cardigan, white socks and classic little navy shoes, but giving her that responsibility meant I had to learn to live with her choice (and with the family photographs afterwards displayed on everyone's mantelpieces!)

Our ultimate goal is to equip our children with the tools and the values they need to make good and wise choices in a world where choices are unlimited. Introducing them to the concept at an early age, will help flex, develop, and build their decision-making muscles as the years go by. And it will help them, and us, be ready for the day when the choices they must make are far more significant.

There will undoubtedly be some mistakes made on the way, but for our children, learning lessons while we are around to pick up the pieces is generally easier than learning them once they have flown the nest and are away from our care. Parent with elastic – its never too soon to start.

"Yeah, it's my mum and dad. They think I don't know they're following me..."

VALUES ARE
MORE OFTEN

CAUGHT

THAN

TAUGHT

Values are more often caught than taught

Visit any company or corporation and in the lift or reception area you are likely to find a list of company values on display. Executives have often spent hours crafting this document, getting the wording exactly right to reflect the heart of their business. But the core value statement is not even worth the paper it is written on unless it is adhered to by the management and employees of the company. If I am kept waiting 30 minutes for a meeting with no explanation, the statement in the lift that 'Our value is to give excellent service and to put the client first' will sound a little hollow. A company's values need to be owned, lived, and embodied by the representatives of the company themselves. The same is true of family values.

We were on the way to football and running late. The children had toasted and eaten the remnants of a loaf of bread after school and there was now no bread for sandwiches for tomorrow. The high street was busy with nowhere to park, so I quickly pulled in on a double yellow line and dashed into the supermarket. Two minutes later, wholemeal loaf (no bits) under my arm, I emerged to see a traffic warden peering in the car window. I gave him a profuse apology, which he graciously accepted with a warning not to repeat the escapade, and we headed off for the match. I thought nothing more of the incident until the evening, when one of our children questioned me in detail about why it had been OK for us to park on double yellow lines.

Their cross examination was worthy of a QC at the Old Bailey, and any futile attempts to justify my position were unconvincing. Guilty as charged. The child had been genuinely perplexed that I had 'broken the law', and I reflected later that evening the truth of the maxim that values are indeed more often 'caught than taught'. His young mind found it hard to distinguish between breaking a rule about parking on a yellow line and breaking a school rule about wearing trainers instead of school shoes or talking in assembly. I had to admit he had a point.

While we need to be real and not pretend to be anything we are not, the truth is that our children are watching. They notice if we stop and buy a *Big Issue* and give the vendor dignity. They notice if we point out if we have been undercharged when paying for something. They notice how we treat our friends, parents, and colleagues. And they notice what we believe about matters of life and death, faith or the environment.

I think of one family who had encouraged their children always to be generous. They had been collecting for a charitable appeal and had urged their offspring to sort through any clothes they had grown out of to donate to the cause. The following day their son came home from school wearing his trainers. He explained that he had given his brand-new school shoes away to a homeless person. As she headed out to buy a new pair before the shops closed, I imagine that mum felt a mixture of exasperation and annoyance, but underpinning it all, a reassuring sense of pride that their family values were getting through.

There is a proverb which says, 'Train up a child in the way he should go: and when he is old he will not depart from it.'[24] Of course, it's not a guarantee, but the truth is that what we sow into our children's lives isn't wasted. We so often worry with our children that 'Nothing is going in!' but the problem can be the opposite: not a word is lost. What we say and do – especially

{ 24 Proverbs 22:6 }

in these primary years – has a profound effect upon their lives, forever. William Wordsworth wrote, 'The child is father of the man'[25] – and he was right: so often what is poured into our lives when we are very young, especially by example, forms character and values that will last down the years.

As our children get older, they may not share our values, but we are their parents and it's important that they know what we believe. If faith is important to us, we will want to hand it on to them. We may want to teach them to pray, but more importantly let them catch us praying; let them see the reality of faith in our lives. We can pass on what we believe about the environment, about relationships, about money or simply about the things that we believe are right and wrong.

If you haven't ever done so, it is worth taking a moment to think what your family values are. What are the things that you believe are important, the non-negotiables that you seek to live by?

A friend recently bought us a black and white picture, which now takes pride of place in our kitchen. It reads:

Have hope.
Be strong.
Play hard.
Live in the moment.
Smile often.
Dream big.
Remember you are loved.
And never, never give up.

25 William Wordsworth, 'My heart leaps up when I behold' in *Poems, in Two Volumes*, Longman, Hurst, Rees and Orme (London, 1807)

If we had designed it ourselves we would no doubt have added some more, but these values are not a bad place to start in giving our family some bearings for life – compass readings that we can return to when the storms of life come our way. But in the same way as a company's values are worthless unless they are owned and embodied, our children will only absorb the family values that they see us living.

The values we live by will be caught rather than taught. We sometimes worry that our children aren't listening to us, but the sobering truth is that not a word or an action is lost.

TAKE A SECOND LOOK

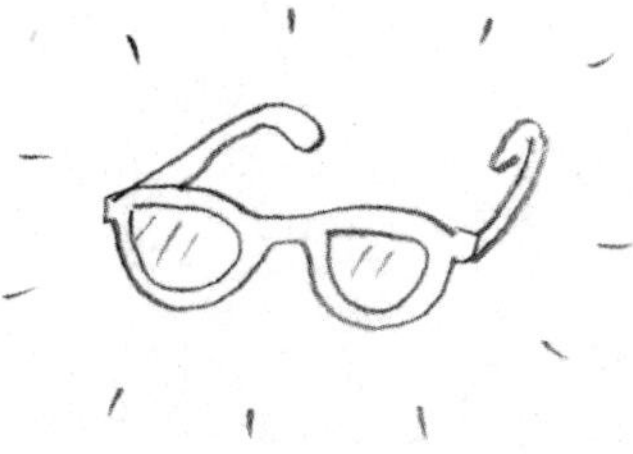

Take a second look

A young girl was sitting in a chemistry lesson at Edgbaston High School. The lesson had only just begun when her teacher burst through the door to break the news that she been awarded the Nobel Peace Prize. At seventeen she was the youngest person ever to have received this honour. Her name is Malala Yousafzai.

Malala was born in Pakistan, and from a young age she campaigned for the right for girls to have an education. She gained an increasing public platform and became well known for her views.

The 9th of October 2012 had been another ordinary school day in the Swat Valley in North-West Pakistan for Malala. She walked out of the school gates as usual and climbed onto a small bus for the short trip home, which would take her past a clearing and along a canal. She squeezed up on the benches with her friends, and they chattered about the day and the exam they had just sat. As the bus passed the clearing, a man flagged it down. Another young man approached the back of the van, and swung onto the tailboard, and leaned in. Brandishing a Colt 45 he shouted to the terrified schoolgirls, 'Who is Malala?'

No one said anything but several of the girls looked at Malala – she was the only one with her face not covered. The gunman shot her at point blank range. The bullet grazed her brain, travelling from above the back of her left eye down the side of her jaw and into her neck. She was in a critical condition, her life hanging in the balance. She had paid the price for her incredible stand for the right of girls to receive an education.

She was flown to a hospital in Peshawar and then brought to Birmingham where she has made an astonishing recovery.

Where did her resilience and courage come from?

In her biography, Malala writes that for most Pashtuns it's a gloomy day when a daughter is born. The day Malala was born, the people in the village commiserated with her mother and nobody congratulated her father.[26]

But her father, Ziauddin, looked into her eyes, then took a longer, second look. He fell in love. This man recognised the potential in his daughter. He told people, 'I know there is something different about this child'. He decided the name that he would give her: Malala means 'heroic freedom fighter.' Then he did something incredible. That second look spurred him on to defy cultural norms. He asked friends to come round to celebrate her birth, and to throw coins into her crib – something that was usually only done for boys. Each coin was a statement of the love and confidence he had in her. Each coin said, 'You have gifts. You have an identity. You have a destiny to fulfil … You are special.'

The affirmation and significance represented by those coins began when she was in her crib but their effect on her has lasted all her life. It has shaped her and has allowed her to become the woman she is today. Secure in her identity, she has become known as 'an icon of courage and hope'.

Malala's father was interviewed about his daughter. He was asked what he had done, as a father, to instil such resilience in her. He replied, 'Don't ask me what I did; ask me what I did not do. I did not clip her wings.'[27]

26 Malala Youosafzai and Christina Lamb, *I am Malala: The Girl Who Stood Up for Education and was Shot by the Taliban*, Terbitan Little, Brown and Company. (New York, 2013) p.9

27 Yousafzai, Ziauddin. (2014) *My Daughter, Malala*. Ted Talks. http://www.ted.com/talks/ziauddin_yousafzai_my_daughter_malala.

He may have not clipped her wings, but of course so much of what Malala became *was* because of the things he *did*. He refused to passively accept what his culture said to him about his daughter's future, and he dared to believe differently. He dared to take a second look. The coins in the crib, the belief that he had in her, gave Malala the message: 'You have value, you *can* stand tall, you are special.'

What an incredible gift to send a child into the world with.

Spot your child's potential. They may not fit into society's definition of success. They may not be great sportsmen or women, they may not be gifted academically, or look the part. They may have learning difficulties or other additional needs that sometimes make life a challenge – but each child is unique and has gifts to offer the world. Spot them and encourage them.

Always take a second look.

SNOW
LEOPARD
MOMENTS

Snow leopard moments

I saw a film recently that has a lovely scene in it. A photographer for a popular magazine desperately wants a picture of a snow leopard. Snow leopards are beautiful animals that live in the mountains of Central and South Asia. They have green eyes and thick, smoky grey fur with dark grey spots, and they are an endangered species.

The photographer's ambition was to capture a picture of this animal. He makes a journey into the mountains, settles down in his tent and waits and waits. A friend has been looking for him and comes and joins him. Days and days go by and there is no sign of this animal. Then, one evening, in a breath-taking moment, the snow leopard appears. Its magnificent form fills the lens of the camera. The friends hold their breath and watch. The snow leopard looks full on at the camera, lingers for 30 seconds, and then disappears back to where he came from. The spell is broken as the friend turns to him astounded and says, 'You didn't take the picture!' The photographer replies in words to this effect, 'It was such an incredible moment, I couldn't do it. I just needed to enjoy the moment.'

We enjoyed that film while on a family holiday in a seaside cottage in Wales. While we were there, we had the use of a couple of sea kayaks and most afternoons we would paddle out through the waves to try to catch some fish. We experimented with different weights, different lines and different bait, but all in vain. By the end of the week, all we had caught was a solitary miniature mackerel. On the final evening, the sun was setting, the sea was calm, and the weather glorious (who needs the Med?), and we decided to give the kayaks one last outing. We had been paddling for about ten minutes when suddenly a fish jumped up just ahead of us, its silver scales catching the light of the setting sun. It was followed by another and then another and another, and before we knew it, we were surrounded by hundreds and hundreds of jumping bass. The sea was teeming. We reached for the lines, but as we did so we felt a check in our spirits. Richard turned to me and said, 'This is a "snow leopard moment". Let's not catch them: let's just enjoy it.'

In our children's lives there are so many snow leopard moments. I can understand that we may want to video their first steps, their starring role in the Nativity play, or their efforts in the final of the egg and spoon race on Sports Day, but sometimes the real place for those things is in our hearts and not on the camera. Have your own 'internal camera' and take time to capture those special times that are often found in the everyday moments of family life. Perhaps it's our little girl tucking her doll in at night; the chocolate-smeared grin of our six-year-old as he polishes off the leftover cupcake icing; or the sight of our children peacefully asleep without a care in the world.

These snow leopard moments are so precious. Watch out for them, and feel and enjoy them to the full. Try not to miss a single one.

Give them roots

On any journey, we need to start with the end in mind. And as parents, when life is all-consuming, it's good sometimes to pause, step back, and remind ourselves that what we are doing now is equipping our children to be secure, confident adults who can go on to fulfil their potential and to build strong relationships themselves in years to come.

A friend once sent me a lovely quote that I have found so helpful over the years. It said this:

There are two things we should give our children, one is roots and the other wings.

In these important, formative years, our focus as parents is to help them put down strong roots that will give them security and strength in the future. We do this by building their character and placing values in their lives. And character and values aren't built overnight. There's a lesson we can learn from the bamboo tree. After the seed for this extraordinary tree is planted in the ground, you see nothing for four years, except for a tiny shoot coming out from the bulb. During those four years, all the energy and growth goes into a huge root system that grows deep and wide under the earth. But then, in the fifth year, the tree grows to eighty feet tall.

As we invest in our children's lives in these primary years, we may not always see the results straight away. We may feel exasperated at our children's behaviour and it can sometimes feel like we are banging our heads against a brick wall. But we can trust that much of the work is being done in secret, underground. Strong roots are growing in their lives that in time will anchor them securely when they navigate the often stormy weather of the teenage years and beyond.

CARPE DIEM

This week's news reported the tragic suicide of the much-loved Hollywood actor Robin Williams. One of the roles for which he will be best remembered is the maverick English teacher, John Keating, in the film *Dead Poets Society*. There's an inspiring scene when he leads the boys out of the classroom and into a corridor lined with row upon row of framed photographs of boys that have gone before. He gathers the class together, looks at the photos and says:

They're not that different from you, are they? Same haircuts. Full of hormones, just like you. Invincible, just like you feel. The world is their oyster. They believe they're destined for great things, just like many of you. Their eyes are full of hope, just like you. Did they wait until it was too late to make from their lives even one iota of what they were capable? Because, you see, gentlemen, these boys are now fertilising daffodils. But if you listen real close, you can hear them whisper their legacy to you. Go on, lean in. Listen, you hear it? … Carpe … hear it? Carpe … Carpe diem. Seize the day, boys. Make your lives extraordinary.

Now, replace that classroom of students and their hopes and dreams with a group of parents and their hopes and dreams – not just for their own lives, but for the lives of their children.

Without a shadow of doubt, John Keating would have whispered the same message – perhaps with even more urgency: *Carpe diem*. Seize the day.

Twenty-six years ago, when Richard and I started out as parents, older and wiser friends would say to me, 'Don't wish the time away; it goes so fast.' And as we have journeyed through the ups and downs of family life – the sleepless nights, the toddler tantrums in the supermarket queue, the first day at school, the roller coaster of the teenage years – I confess there have been many times when I have wanted to do just that and fast-forward to a slower day. But now, as I am standing on the threshold of the empty nest, I see things a little differently and understand the wisdom of that advice.

Some time ago, a mum said to me, 'I hear people talk about the empty nest. At the moment I've got a baby that won't stop crying, a two-year-old that is determined to feed Weetabix to her hamster and a teenager that seems to have lost the ability to speak: that empty nest sounds pretty attractive!' I sympathise. And yet even as she spoke, my mind went to something I'd heard another mother say some years ago:

'Remember that bedroom strewn with crisp packets, scrunched up homework, muddy sports kit, damp towels, odd socks (and shoes!) and enough dirty underwear to start an epidemic? Of course you do. You have yelled for it to be tidied, bribed for it to be tidied and prayed for it to be tidied. Well one day it will be – too tidy!

You'll be free! No more birthday cakes to make in the shape of cartoon characters, nativity costumes to conjure up using old curtains and a tea towel and no more solemn goldfish burials in the garden. You'll have time to yourself:

no buggies to manoeuvre into overcrowded shops, no haircuts with a wriggling toddler on your knee, no four-year-olds wandering half asleep into your bedroom, no leaving a drink for Father Christmas, no knotted hair after swimming, no trying to skip pages reading a bedtime story and getting found out.

Honey sandwiches, hide and seek, stories under the sheets, tonsils, school runs, shoe laces, lunch boxes, croup, milk teeth, cut knees, first periods and maths periods – all gone. Bringing up young children will be all done and dusted.

One day you'll say 'It's time you kids grew up!'

And they will.

The years of childhood do go by so quickly. Don't wish the time away, be kind to yourself, lay down regrets. Tonight, even if you are so tired you think you can barely keep your eyes open a moment longer, just pause. Take a moment to look back over today. Find something, however small, to celebrate, to enjoy. And look ahead to tomorrow and resolve to do the same. Make the most of every moment that you can. *Carpe diem.*

And take heart – nobody knows your child like you – and nobody loves them like you. Have confidence in your parenting. There is no one way to be a *perfect* parent – but there are a hundred ways to be a *great* parent. There is no task more important than bringing up the next generation – enjoy!

If you forget everything else, remember this.